PUB STROLLS IN
NORTHAMPTONSHIRE

Judy Smith

COUNTRYSIDE BOOKS
NEWBURY BERKSHIRE

First published 2002
© Judy Smith 2002

COUNTRYSIDE BOOKS
3 Catherine Road
Newbury, Berkshire

To view our complete range of books,
please visit us at
www.countrysidebooks.co.uk

ISBN 1 85306 729 6

Designed by Graham Whiteman

Typeset by Techniset Typesetters, Newton-le-Willows
Produced through MRM Associates Ltd., Reading
Printed in Italy

Contents

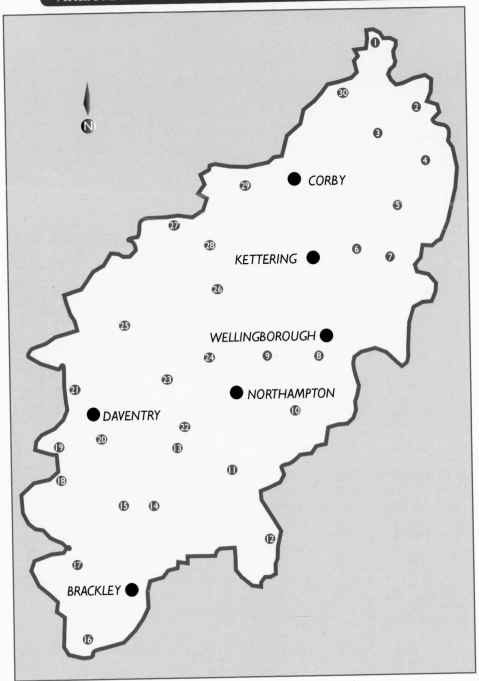

PUBLISHER'S NOTE

We hope that you obtain considerable enjoyment from this book; great care has been taken in its preparation. Although at the time of publication all routes followed public rights of way or permitted paths, diversion orders can be made and permissions withdrawn.

We cannot, of course, be held responsible for such diversion orders and any inaccuracies in the text which result from these or any other changes to the routes nor any damage which might result from walkers trespassing on private property. We are anxious though that all details covering the walks are kept up to date and would therefore welcome information from readers which would be relevant to future editions.

The simple sketch maps that accompany the walks in this book are based on notes made by the author whilst checking out the routes on the ground. They are designed to show you how to reach the start, to point out the main features of the overall circuit and they contain a progression of numbers that relate to the paragraphs of the text.

However, for the benefit of a proper map, we do recommend that you purchase the relevant Ordnance Survey sheet covering your walk. The Ordnance Survey maps are widely available, especially through booksellers and local newsagents.

Pub strolling – the art of taking just a short amble combined with perhaps a more extended meal – is as popular today as it ever has been. And with an abundance of excellent hostelries and a varied but gentle landscape, Northamptonshire must be the ideal county in which to practise it!

So what are the ingredients of a good pub stroll? Taking the walk first, Northamptonshire has plenty to offer. The county is perhaps best known for its lovely old villages and some of the best are included here. In the north, Easton-on-the-Hill is a village of silver-grey limestone where many of the houses are listed buildings, and honey-stone Yarwell was once the home of stonemasons. Farther south, Wadenhoe was 'apparently made in heaven' according to one text. Then there are the beautifully preserved estate villages: Ashton and Apethorpe, Great Brington and Chapel Brampton. Extending into the countryside, the west side of the county around Badby and Hellidon boasts the attractive rolling landscape of the Northamptonshire Heights, while farther south near Chacombe and Aynho the hills are softened and form the edge of the Cotswolds. In the east, the landscape of the winding Nene Valley is enriched by pretty riverside villages, each topped with a grey church spire. Gravel extraction in the Nene Valley has left many lakes, which are particularly popular with migrating wildfowl – and ideal for a gentle stroll around the banks. Through the heart of the county runs the Grand Union Canal, the main artery of Britain's waterways, always busy and exciting and with a good towpath alongside.

And what of the pubs in this book? It has been an experience visiting so many! In the end, many of those included are smaller family-run establishments, where even though the menu may not be quite so extensive, the food is home-made and the atmosphere friendly. Character and individuality make them worth seeking out – pubs with low beams and roaring log fires in winter, pubs so old they were visited by Cromwell's soldiers en route to Naseby, pubs that are amazingly good value, pubs with idiosyncratic décor, pubs beside the river or canal, pubs with outstandingly exotic menus even though they are miles from anywhere, pubs with delightful beer gardens – and always pubs welcoming children. Traditionally, many also welcome man's best friend, his dog, into the bar area. Each pub asked was pleased for pattrons to leave their cars while walking – but it would be courtesy just to ask someone first. If you decide to opt for roadside parking instead, do be careful not to block any exits or entrances.

So now you are ready to go pub strolling. All you will need is a pair of stout shoes on your feet, and perhaps the relevant Ordnance Survey map to help you round. The new Explorer maps are very clear and good value for money. The routes here are all short and present no particular difficulties. A good pub awaits you at the end - and if you have yet more energy, there are also suggestions for places to visit nearby.

In conclusion, my thanks go to those who helped with this book – to our friends Richard and Margaret for their hospitality and of course, to my husband Eric, who accompanied me all the way.

Judy Smith

Easton-on-the-Hill
The Oak Inn

MAP: OS LANDRANGER 141 OR EXPLORER 234 (GR 011040)

WALK 1

DISTANCE: 4 MILES

DIRECTIONS TO START: EASTON-ON-THE-HILL IS ON THE A43 KETTERING ROAD, 2 MILES SOUTH OF STAMFORD. THE OAK IS BESIDE THAT ROAD AT THE SOUTHERN END OF THE VILLAGE. **PARKING:** AT THE OAK FOR PATRONS OR ON QUIET ROADSIDES IN THE VILLAGE.

Here is a walk visiting three counties, and teeming with interest all the way. It starts at Easton, a beautiful hilltop village of old limestone houses under Collyweston slate roofs. More than 40 of them are listed buildings! The oldest is the tiny 15th century Priest's House, cared for by the National Trust, while nearby the 300 year old Glebe House was once the home of Captain Skynner of the ship *Lutine*. The famous Lutine Bell is now kept at Lloyd's in London and traditionally rung when a ship is lost at sea.

The walk takes you down the hill to the River Welland, and there are fine views of Stamford as you go. Later following a pleasant path along the banks of the winding river, you can visit the site of Stamford Spa, a spring said to have had remarkable healing properties. A mill at the riverside comes before the broad uphill track to Easton, passing another fine building, the Keeper's Lodge built by the Marquis of Exeter in 1845.

The Oak Inn

This is a handsome old building in the characteristic village stone. Inside, the atmosphere is surprisingly light and airy – partly as a result of the conservatory-like restaurant on one side, and also because the furniture, floor and bar are all of light pine. Informal meals are generally taken in the bar, which has plenty of comfortable seating.

The Oak is actually a small country hotel, but, nonetheless, is particularly welcoming to walkers. The lunchtime menu is quite comprehensive – from triple-decker sandwiches, hot baguettes, pasta and salads through to a two-course steak dinner. Steaks are something of a speciality – try Julienne of Rump au Poivre, batons of rump steak cooked in peppercorn sauce with cream and brandy. The evening menu in the restaurant is more formal and extensive. This is a free house and there is a good range of beers and a choice of real ales to accompany the meal. The Oak serves food both at lunchtime and in the evening every day except Mondays. Children are welcome – and dogs could be admitted on the approval of the owner's terrier! Telephone: 01780 752286.

The Walk

① From the Oak Inn, turn left and immediately left again down Porter's Lane. At the crossroads, turn right and pass the Blue Bell. Turn left at the war memorial (Church Street). Now you can enjoy the superb old houses (and their

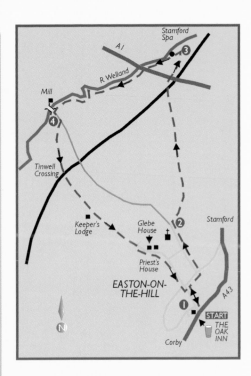

curious names) as you dip and then climb to the church.

② At the end of the tarmacked road, take a footpath on the right, the route of both the Jurassic Way and the Macmillan Way. The path crosses behind Easton House, and then runs across the corner of a field. Keeping the same direction in the next field, you arrive at the top corner of a third field. Continue on the broad path to the right of the hedge (the first small tree in this hedge is a rare Midland Thorn). The path descends through woodland, crosses a field, and climbs steps to the railway. Cross with care (the little sprinter trains here look delightfully like blue-nosed caterpillars) and bear right across the next field to an arch under the A1. Now you are in Lincolnshire. The track

Easton village

continues across the grassy field to the riverside.

③ Turn to the left and follow the riverside path — soon you pass the site of Stamford Spa. The path is a pleasant one and you can enjoy half an hour's walk along the bank. After passing under the A1 again you are in Rutland. Look behind you as you go for a good view of Wothorpe Towers projecting from the hillside — it was built in the 17th century for Thomas Cecil, Earl of Exeter. He lived at nearby Burghley House, but apparently needed somewhere to take refuge at times of spring cleaning! At length you reach a fingerpost beside a bridge – the fine complex on the right was once an old mill.

④ Turn left on the path beside the hedge. At its end (150 yards) turn right on a narrow track between hedges. This widens and crosses the railway (more care!) before climbing past the Keeper's Lodge. Arriving at Easton at the top of the hill, keep ahead on the road, passing the Glebe House and the Priest's House. Soon you arrive again at the crossroads you passed earlier and cross straight over to return to the Oak.

PLACES OF INTEREST NEARBY

Stamford is a town of perfectly preserved Georgian buildings. Park your car at the riverside and simply wander at will!

Yarwell
The Angel

MAP: OS LANDRANGER 142 OR EXPLORER 15 (234) (GR 071978)

WALK 2

DISTANCE: 3$\frac{1}{2}$ MILES

DIRECTIONS TO START: TURN OFF THE A605 JUST NORTH OF OUNDLE, SIGNED TO COTTERSTOCK, AND CONTINUE THROUGH FOTHERINGHAY AND NASSINGTON TO YARWELL. THE ANGEL IS IN THE MAIN STREET OPPOSITE THE CHURCH. **PARKING:** ON QUIET ROADSIDES IN THE VILLAGE – THE ANGEL PUB DOES NOT HAVE ITS OWN CAR PARK.

The little village of Yarwell was once a centre for stonemasons – it must have been a pleasure to work with the lovely honey-coloured limestone found in this area. The walk from here takes you through watermeadows beside the now wide River Nene on its way to the county boundary at Wansford. On the way it is possible to visit Simsey Island, the largest island in the river.

Reaching the elegant bridge at Wansford, you can simply continue home beside the quiet road. A more exciting choice is the path through Old Sulehay Forest, ancient woodland renowned for its abundant wild flowers. And the path returns across the site of an old stone quarry that is now a conservation area — the vegetation growing on the exposed limestone is a treasure trove for any botanist.

The Angel

Pubs like this are the salt of the earth! The tiny stone-built Angel has been serving the people of Yarwell for around 300 years. There have been a few extensions and alterations over time, but it is still today a meeting place for villagers. In summer, their numbers are augmented by those who make the $\frac{1}{2}$ mile or so trek from the camping site and boat moorings at Yarwell Mill.

The interior of the Angel is homely, a place of low beams, horse-brasses and simple décor. A log-burning stove, housed in its handsome stone fireplace, offers warmth and comfort in winter. Lunchtime food here is simple – merely rolls and sandwiches, but they are well presented. In the evening (7 pm onwards) you can enjoy steaks, fish, vegetarian dishes and the like – all wholesome food, well cooked. The choice is likely to be greater in the summertime to cater for the visitors. This is a free house and a suitable range of beverages is on offer to accompany the meal. The friendly owners are happy to welcome both children and dogs inside, but there is also a small garden to the rear. Telephone: 01780 782582.

The Walk

① From the Angel, turn left down the village street. As the road bends right, take a footpath on the left – you are now on the Nene Way and have only to follow its signs across the fields to reach Wansford. (Over to the right you can see the guillotine on the lock beside Simsey Island – follow the direction of the

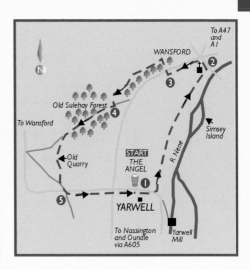

fingerpost if you want to take a detour.) Approaching Wansford you cross a wide watermeadow with fine views of the old bridge (1795). Climbing on a path beside a horse paddock you reach the road.

② To the right is the bridge and, beyond, the village of Wansford – a blend of hostelries and curiosity shops begging exploration! But this route turns left towards the church and left again at the road junction. The road first dips and then climbs. Pass the doctors' surgery and two houses, then look for a stile in the stone wall to the right.

③ This footpath leads you through woodland beside a low stone wall. Emerging from the trees, turn left and follow the field edge to reach a gate leading into Old Sulehay Forest. Continue through the forest for a couple of minutes to reach a junction.

④ Turn right, now on the main track through the wood. The track widens and climbs gently through the luxurious

Wansford bridge on the River Nene

vegetation. After a clearing with a huge chestnut tree, there is a deep water-filled quarry on the left and then another quarry at the level of your path. At a wide gap in the hedge, turn left to enter the quarry. Take the centre of the three paths facing you, and coming to a hillock, bear left and ahead on a path through clumps of silver birch. The path bears right, and at a fork, you see a Conservation Area board ahead. Turn left opposite the board, cross the stile, and follow the path to the road.

⑤ Turn left on the road to reach Yarwell beside its fine village sign. Cross the main

road and walk down the village street to return to the Angel.

PLACES OF INTEREST NEARBY

At nearby **Nassington**, the 13th century **Prebendal Manor** (1230) is the oldest inhabited house in Northamptonshire. It is open on Wednesdays, Sundays and bank holidays from May to September. Telephone: 01780 782575. And just a few miles north is perhaps the most splendid sight in the Nene valley – the exquisite church at **Fotheringhay**, with its lantern tower looking out over the river. A nearby mound is all that remains of Fotheringhay Castle, where Mary Queen of Scots was executed.

Apethorpe
The King's Head

DIRECTIONS TO START: JUST NORTH OF DEENE PARK ON THE A43 BETWEEN CORBY AND STAMFORD, TURN OFF EASTWARDS, SIGNED TO BLATHERWYCKE AND KING'S CLIFFE. KEEP RIGHT IN KING'S CLIFFE AND CONTINUE THROUGH TO APETHORPE. THE KING'S HEAD IS ON THE RIGHT AS YOU ARRIVE.
PARKING: AT THE KING'S HEAD FOR PATRONS OR ON QUIET ROADSIDES IN THE VILLAGE.

Apethorpe Hall was first owned by Sir Walter Mildmay, Chancellor of the Exchequer under Elizabeth I, and later came into the possession of the Earls of Westmorland. Apethorpe village belonged to that estate. Before or after your walk, take a stroll down to the village centre where the 15th century church stands beside the old grey hall and the village stocks are preserved for posterity in their niche in the wall opposite.

Across the fields from Apethorpe lies King's Cliffe, a handsome village of Northamptonshire stone, which in medieval times was an important settlement in the vast Rockingham Forest. Tracts of this ancient woodland remain today, and through the timeless landscape the little Willow Brook hurries on its way to join the Nene – all in all, a most pleasant setting for this short ramble.

The King's Head

A fine old stone building, the King's Head is in keeping with the rest of this lovely estate village. Inside, its lounge bar and large restaurant area are tastefully decorated with plentiful restored natural wood and many old photographs of Apethorpe Hall and other local properties. Outside, there is a small courtyard area with stone seats, a pleasant place on a hot day.

The menu here is a gourmet's delight, including such delicacies as wild boar and apple sausages and Wiltshire hog (simmered in cider with rosemary and cream). There is also an imaginative and popular 'lighter snack' menu from which you can choose various deep-fried morsels (fish, vegetables etc) along with salad. Vegetarians are particularly well catered for. Drinks to accompany your meal include Scrumpy Jack, Adnams Broadside, Greene King IPA and a guest beer. The King's Head serves food every day both at lunchtime and in the evening. Children are welcome in the restaurant and food can also be served in the bar area, ideal for dog owners. Telephone: 01780 470627.

The Walk

① Take the hard-surfaced track that runs uphill beside the King's Head. Ignore the left turn (this goes to Lodge Farm) and continue ahead for about ³/₄ mile, to reach Spa Farm Cottages where the road swings left.

② Keep straight ahead on the footpath under the trees. At the track junction on the edge of the wood, keep straight ahead beside the hedge — you can see King's Cliffe across the fields. Maintain this direction along the edge of three fields to reach a green lane (Morehay Lane)

③ Turn left on this lane. In about 200 yards, take a footpath on the right. This passes through an interesting hilly area and descends to cross Willow Brook. On the far side is a tarmacked lane, on which you turn to the right.

④ The lane comes out beside the church (look for William Law's tomb – see Places of Interest Nearby). Turn right (away from the main road) and continue downhill, bearing left at the grassy triangle. At the end of the lane, a track takes you into the field and over Willow Brook to join Morehay Lane again. Turn left along the lane.

⑤ In about 100 yards, take the footpath on the right, heading uphill beside the hedge. Look backwards as you go for some fine views of King's Cliffe. At the top of the hill, the path continues across an old clay pit on a sort of raised ridge. Bearing slightly to the right, you descend into a

PLACES OF INTEREST NEARBY

William Law, theologian, writer and philosopher, was born in **King's Cliffe** in 1686. His tomb in the churchyard is topped with a large stone writing desk. At nearby **Woodnewton** the churchyard contains a rather more surprising gravestone – far from his native Russia, here sleeps Nicolai Poliakovs, Coco the Clown.

Willow Brook at King's Cliffe

dip. To leave it, cross the stile (waymarked) and continue beside the hedge and then across fields. You can't go wrong – the King's Head is in view all the way! Reaching the stony road again, turn left to complete the journey.

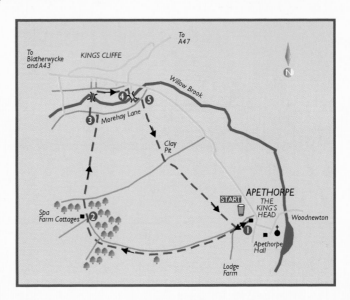

Ashton
The Chequered Skipper

MAP: OS LANDRANGER 141 AND 142 OR EXPLORER 227 (GR 057883)

WALK 4

DISTANCE: 4 MILES

DIRECTIONS TO START: AT THE ROUNDABOUT ON THE A605 JUST NORTH OF OUNDLE, TURN SOUTH-EAST (SIGNPOSTED TO POLEBROOK). IN ABOUT ½ MILE, TURN LEFT WHERE SIGNPOSTED TO ASHTON. THE CHEQUERED SKIPPER IS BESIDE THE GREEN. **PARKING:** AROUND THE GREEN AND BESIDE THE PUB.

Ashton village is quite unique – a score of mock-Tudor thatched cottages surround a green shaded by horse chestnuts. The pub is in matching style. It is a chocolate box scene that has remained unchanged since 1900, when this estate village was rebuilt by Charles Rothschild of nearby Ashton Wold. His employees were well provided for, as each house was supplied with water and electricity (generated by Lord Rothschild himself at nearby Ashton Mill), and even had the luxury of a bathroom! Ashton has another claim to fame. Each autumn it hosts the World Conker Championships – an event that is by no means just child's play!

From Ashton, this walk takes you through the peaceful watermeadows beside the River Nene and returns you through Oundle town with its many interesting old houses. Oundle church spire, the tallest and most elegant in Northamptonshire, is in view all the way.

The Chequered Skipper

Lord Rothschild was particularly interested in butterflies and named the village pub after his favourite – the chequered skipper. The species is sadly now extinct. The pub is splendidly situated beside the village green, which serves as its beer garden! Tables are scattered under the chestnut trees and peacocks from Ashton Wold wander at will in this olde worlde setting. Inside, however, all is modern and bright! The Chequered Skipper was severely damaged by fire some few years back, and has been rebuilt. There is now a Scandinavian feel to the attractive light wood furniture and beams, enhanced in the restaurant by the polished wooden floor, open fireplace and wrought iron candlesticks.

The food here is as excellent as it sounds (braised pork loin steak with cider, apricots and aubergines is delicious – and try Bailey's cheesecake to follow), and, in keeping with the surroundings, it is stylishly served. But you can opt for lesser fare. Baguettes and jackets have a variety of exotic fillings – and summer weekends offer a lunchtime barbecue. Children are very welcome inside and out, and dogs are plainly at home in the bar area. Food is served every lunchtime and evening, and a variety of real ales, particularly local brews, is on offer. Telephone: 01832 273494.

The Walk

① From the Chequered Skipper, cross the green and follow the Nene Way signs along the path beside the chapel wall.

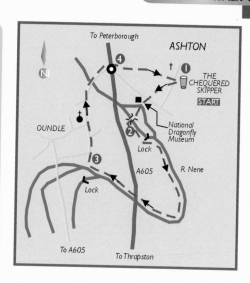

Cross the field with its fine views of the lovely crocketed spire of St Peter's, and descend to the road. Turn right for about 50 yards to reach the National Dragonfly Museum at Ashton Mill – if it's open you should return later (see Places of Interest Nearby). Now continue between the mill buildings and take the track leading to a metal bridge over the Nene.

② Cross the bridge, turn left and follow the river bank. On your left water gushes over the sluice and Ashton Lock is hidden in the trees. The path crosses a field alongside the lock, but soon returns to the river bank. The way is now straightforward – a lovely grassy track beside the lazy curving river. Wild geese graze the fields while herons stand silently at the water's edge. In summer, waterlilies drift in the shallows. After about a mile you pass under the road bridge (once a railway bridge) and continue beside the river under the trees. Crossing an open field with pollarded willows, you reach a metal footbridge.

The River Nene near Ashton

③ Turn right here (leaving the Nene Way) and cross the field. Through the gate, walk up the road and turn right at its end. Soon you reach Oundle town square with the old town hall at its centre. Opposite is the church, and all around are the houses of Oundle School. Continue ahead on North Street, passing some fine old buildings, including Latham's Hospital dating from 1611. Leaving the town, you cross the river and reach a roundabout on the A605.

④ Cross to the bank opposite where a footpath sign directs you to climb uphill with the hedge on your left. Pass through a little patch of woodland and continue uphill. A stile leads you into an open field and you head for the stone wall at the top. Here another stile takes you into the chapel grounds and, crossing through, you are once again on Ashton green.

PLACES OF INTEREST NEARBY

The **National Dragonfly Museum** is a fascinating place. Inside are exhibitions, videos, larvae tanks and so on, while out of doors on a sunny day you can see the real thing in action in a variety of watery habitats. The museum is open from June to September (weekends only). Telephone: 01832 272427. And while you are here, take a few minutes to look around **Oundle** with its fine old buildings, antique shops and tearooms. The crocketed spire of St Peter's church is Northamptonshire's highest at 208 ft.

Wadenhoe
The King's Head

DIRECTIONS TO START: TURN WESTWARDS OFF THE A605 AT THORPE WATERVILLE, 2 MILES NORTH OF THRAPSTON. CONTINUE THROUGH ALDWINCLE, AND IN 1 MILE, TURN RIGHT INTO WADENHOE. KEEP RIGHT IN THE VILLAGE AND DESCEND TOWARDS THE RIVER TO REACH THE KING'S HEAD. **PARKING:** AT THE KING'S HEAD (PATRONS) OR IN THE CAR PARK AT THE BOTTOM OF THE HILL BESIDE THE RIVER.

Wadenhoe is a strong contender for Northamptonshire's most picturesque village! Thatch-roofed mellow stone cottages tumble downhill to a peaceful riverside scene. Nearby, a little grey Norman church stands alone on its own grassy hillock – an invitation to climb, explore and enjoy its view along the valley. Surprisingly, this village once boasted the first postal telegraph office outside London – established here in 1868 by Sir George Ward-Hunt, Chancellor of the Exchequer under Disraeli, who lived in Wadenhoe House. The old enamel sign still hangs above the post office door.

The walk from Wadenhoe takes you past a beautifully restored watermill to wander in watermeadows renowned for their wild flowers, and to ramble through woods above a lock on the river – a fine circuit to be combined with the excellent cuisine of the King's Head.

The King's Head

This lovely old thatched hostelry has the most idyllic setting – its gardens sweep down to the riverside and look out to Wadenhoe Lock. Moorings are provided for boaters and a summer's evening will usually see two or three crews enjoying their well-earned pints. The gardens are well provided with tables and there is also a balcony from which to survey the scene! Inside, the King's Head has all the atmosphere you might expect. The bar area is in two parts, low-beamed, and furnished simply in pine. At the far end of the building is a small cosy restaurant.

Chalkboards around the bar proclaim the menu – and it is a delight to read. For lunch you might try salmon, prawn and crab cakes with wine, honey and mustard dressing – but if you can resist that, even the sandwiches have exotic fillings. In the evening it could be venison or roast pheasant. Ales to go with it all include Adnams Bitter, Adnams Broadside and Fuller's London Pride – and, of course, there is a good wine list. The King's Head serves food every lunchtime and on Wednesday, Thursday, Friday and Saturday evenings. Children are welcome – and even dogs can find a corner in the bar. Telephone: 01832 720024.

The Walk

① Leaving the King's Head, walk uphill, away from the riverside. At the top of the hill, follow the Nene Way signs and turn immediately right to descend Mill Lane. At its end, the path continues ahead on a wooden bridge over a branch of the river – to the right is the beautifully restored old Wadenhoe Mill. The path heads left, but soon bears right to cross the main river on a raised footbridge. These watermeadows are a haven for waterfowl and are a designated Site of Special Scientific Interest. The path now climbs to reach the church of St John the Baptist at Achurch, and passes right through the churchyard. At its far side is a carved oak lychgate, dated 1896.

② Continue along the track for about 100 yards, and then follow the Nene Way signs, turning left into the woodland known as The Linches. A pleasant broad track leads between the trees and soon a sort of junction is reached. Here turn left and continue down steps and along a much narrower path. Lilford Lock can be seen through the trees before you emerge on the road.

③ Turn left on the road and cross two bridges over the river. On the far side, take the footpath diagonally across the field on the left and maintain the direction across a second field to reach a road.

PLACES OF INTEREST NEARBY

Titchmarsh Nature Reserve is an extensive area of lakes along the course of the Nene between Aldwincle and Thrapston. A haven for wildlife of all kinds throughout the year, it is also much favoured as a refuelling stop for wildfowl on their migrations. Access can be gained from Lowick Lane car park at Aldwincle, 2 miles south of Wadenhoe. And while in Aldwincle, look out for **Dryden House** opposite All Saints' church. The poet John Dryden was born here in 1631.

A dovecote at Wadenhoe House passed on the walk

④ Turn left and follow the road back into Wadenhoe. The spire at Achurch now stands prominently across the river. On entering the village you will pass Wadenhoe House (now a conference centre) and on its far side, a circular dovecote. A few paces further along, at the road junction, turn left (the post office with its 'Postal Telegraph Office' sign is to the right), and then bear right down the hill to return to the King's Head.

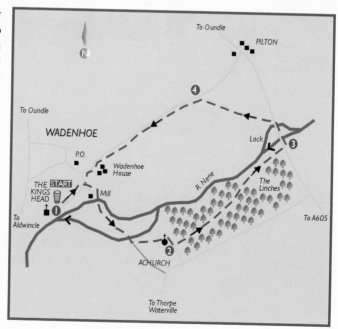

Twywell
The Old Friar

| MAP: OS LANDRANGER 141 OR EXPLORER 224 (GR 954782) | **WALK 6** | DISTANCE: 2 MILES – BUT THERE ARE SHORTER OPTIONS |

DIRECTIONS TO START: TWYWELL LIES 2 MILES WEST OF THRAPSTON, JUST NORTH OF THE A14. THE OLD FRIAR IS AT THE ENTRANCE TO THE VILLAGE. **PARKING:** AT THE OLD FRIAR (PATRONS). THE WALK CAN ALSO BE STARTED FROM THE CAR PARK AT MAIN ENTRANCE TO TWYWELL HILLS AND DALES COUNTRY PARK, OFF THE A14 AT ITS JUNCTION WITH THE A510 – SEE MAP TO JOIN ROUTE AT SIGNPOST (POINT 3).

The land south of Twywell was quarried for iron ore until the 1940s. Now the scars have healed leaving undulating terrain which has recently been incorporated into a most attractive country park – named, aptly enough, Twywell Hills and Dales. You can discover its history on this pleasant ramble over the 'hills', with a contrasting return through the woods.

The walk starts from Twywell, itself a place with a story. In the 1870s, Twywell's rector, the Reverend Waller, was a friend of David Livingstone. When the great explorer died, his heart was buried in Africa, while his body was embalmed, wrapped in bark and carried to England by two natives. Livingstone was subsequently laid to rest in Westminster Abbey, but the bark wrapping was taken to Twywell. The pieces of bark are still displayed in Twywell church, where carvings of elephant and rhino decorate the choirstalls.

The Old Friar

This handsome building of old mellowed stone stands at the lower end of the village. Inside the atmosphere is cosy, and enhanced by low ceilings, flag floors, beams, open fireplaces and soft lighting. There is a reputation for good food here and the Sunday carvery is particularly popular – it has now been extended to include Friday and Saturday nights as well. If it is lesser fare you are seeking, in addition to the usual snacks there are grills, fish, pies, curries and a lot more. Vegetarians are well catered for with a wider-than-usual choice of interesting dishes – try aubergine and two cheese melt or spinach and red pepper lasagne. Children are welcomed with their own menu – and there is a small garden with play area.

Food is served at the Old Friar every lunchtime (except Monday) from 12 noon to 2 pm and a little later at weekends. Evening meals are available from 7 pm to 9.30 pm every day. This is a free house – real ales are John Smith's cask, Courage Directors and Marston's Pedigree along with a guest ale. Telephone: 01832 732625.

The Walk

① From the Old Friar, walk only about 20 yards in the direction of the village and turn left down a gravelled track between houses. The track becomes grassy, and you then take a narrow footpath between hedges on the right. Reaching the small field, keep to the left hand edge to another gate. Through it, turn immediately right and follow the right

PLACES OF INTEREST NEARBY
Heading north-west through Grafton Underwood, you will come to the gates of **Boughton House**, the home of the Duke of Buccleuch. The extensive parkland (with rustic adventure playground) is open to the public every afternoon except Friday from May to mid-September. The house itself, renowned for its fine art collection, is open only in August. Telephone: 01536 417255.

hand boundary of the big field. At the end of the wall, go ahead and cross a stile. Now bear diagonally left to a gate you can see in the distant fence, crossing a small stream in the centre of the field on the way (there is a dry path).

② Turn left and keep the hedge on your left through two fields. At the end of the second, a stile admits you to the Hills and Dales Country Park. Turn right, and in about 15 yards bear left. At a fork, an arrow directs you left to 'Whitestones' – you are now on one of the park trails. At a crosstracks, go right (still following Whitestones) and immediately cross over a broad grassy track and bear left. A deep gully now lies on the right. There are two seats, and a display board tells you all about the quarrying. Still following Whitestones, continue first beside the gully and then down steps on the left. You arrive at a curious piece of carved stone with inlaid birds and flowers. Turn left here, and at the next crosstracks (30 yards approx), turn right. Continue across the grass to a wooden signpost at a woodland corner ahead.

③ Keep straight on here (following Gullet and Woodland). In the wooded

In the Twywell Hills and Dales Country Park

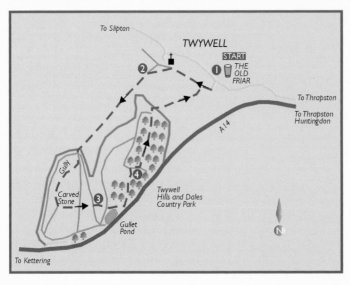

Follow this very pleasant elevated track to arrive at the edge of the wood.

④ Now turn right, and in about 20 yards left, into the wood. At least three grassy rides cross your path, but keep straight ahead at every junction. Eventually the path goes down steps to a gate at the woodland edge. Cross the field ahead, aiming for a sycamore on a small hillock on the right. Just past it, go up the steps and retrace your route to the Old Friar.

gullet, bear round to the right following the red arrow of the Gullet and Woodland Trail. With the A14 ahead, the path bends left and climbs up the ridge.

Ringstead
The Axe and Compass

MAP: OS LANDRANGER 141 OR EXPLORER 224 (GR 984752)

WALK 7

DISTANCE: 1½ MILES WITH 2 MILE EXTENSION POSSIBLE

DIRECTIONS TO START: TURN NORTHWARDS OFF THE A45 JUST NORTH OF RAUNDS (THE SECOND ROUNDABOUT AFTER THE A6 JUNCTION, IF APPROACHING FROM THE SOUTH). AT THE T-JUNCTION IN RINGSTEAD, TURN LEFT AND THEN SECOND RIGHT (CARLOW ROAD) TO FIND THE AXE AND COMPASS. **PARKING:** AT THE AXE AND COMPASS (PATRONS) OR AT THE CAR PARK FOR KINEWELL LAKE, OFF THE ROAD TO GREAT ADDINGTON.

At Ringstead in the Nene valley, Kinewell Lake caters for all the family with this classic pre- or post-lunch stroll. The very oldest can simply sit on the benches looking out over the water while everyone else makes the circuit, and as for the youngest — well, it's so short you can carry them. And if you need more exercise, there's a very pleasant extension.

Kinewell is one of many lakes left after the gravel extractions of some 30 years ago. Willows and alders overhang the banks of bullrushes while various wildfowl dabble in the shallow water. Farther out are islands where many nest. The River Nene runs alongside, and you can admire the colourful boats moored by the old grey watermill. Take your time on this walk – there's lots to see!

The Axe and Compass

In recent years the Axe and Compass has undergone a transformation. Northamptonshire stone from cottages demolished nearby has been used to extend and reconstruct this old hostelry which now has a light and airy restaurant with a conservatory. Meals can also be taken in the large bar area, which presents a total contrast – it retains the atmosphere of a village 'local' with darts, skittles and, in winter, a roaring open fire. And for fine days (or if you have a dog), there's a garden with children's swings.

Wherever you choose to eat, you won't be disappointed with the fare! The bar and garden menu offers 'quick and easy meals at affordable prices' – including steaks topped with Stilton and a delightful vegetarian platter. The restaurant has both table d'hôte and à la carte menus, and the food is as delicious as it sounds. The set price option is justly very popular and is served at lunchtime on Tuesday to Friday and on Tuesday to Saturday evenings. Bar meals are available every lunchtime (12 noon to 2.30 pm) except Monday and every evening (6 pm to 9 pm). A suitably extensive range of ales and wines complements the cuisine. Telephone: 01933 622227.

PLACES OF INTEREST NEARBY

Several riverside areas around Ringstead have open access under the agreement with the Countryside Commission. Taking the extension to this walk, you arrive on Ringstead Island, all of which is open for you to wander. The meadow between Brightwells Lake and the river is similarly accessible and has a fine show of wild flowers in springtime. Yet another 'open' area of lakes is reached via the track behind Willy Watt Mill.

area, and then the hide and picnic table. Continue to the top corner, where the path dives into the trees beside the shore.

② Here you can make a choice – continue on the obvious path around the lake or add a couple of miles to your journey and see the riverside (and another lake) as well. *For the latter, go now to the extension directions at the end.* For the short walk, simply continue along the path, which climbs out of the trees and again follows the shore parallel to a road.

③ At the end of this stretch, the riverside

The Walk

① From the pub, cross the road and walk down Meadow Close. A fingerpost directs you left on a public footpath, which soon arrives at Kinewell Lake. Now turn left and follow the lakeshore all the way, passing the display board by the parking

Upper Ringstead Lock on the Nene

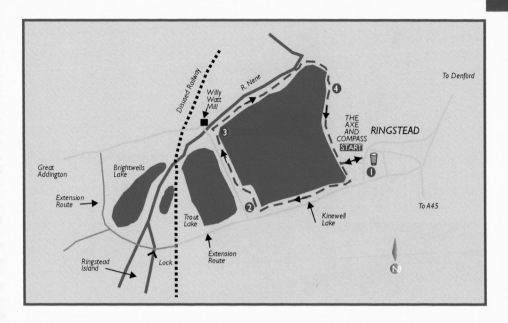

with the grey-stone Willy Watt Mill is directly ahead of you. A stile to the left leads you onto the road if you want to explore – the old millwheel is still beside the building. Across the road is Lower Ringstead Lock with its guillotine gate – hard work for boaters! Back at the lakeside, the path now runs between lake and river. Crossing over the connecting channel, the path soon turns again and crosses a little bay.

④ The next section of the path is gravelled, and separated from the lake by a belt of trees. At its end, a stream enters – a popular spot for sighting kingfishers. After this you are back on the broad grassy area where you first reached the lake – and can retrace your steps to the Axe and Compass.

Extension

From point 2, turn left on the track up to the road. Turn left, and then right (signposted to Great Addington). Follow the road straight ahead for $^1/_2$ mile to cross the river beside Upper Ringstead Lock. You are now on Ringstead Island – an island with its own central lake. Continue across a wooden bridge to reach another lake (Brightwells). Bear right around its shore (lake on your right) and ignore all tracks on the left until you come to a broad track going uphill. This climbs to a road, where you turn right and continue for $^1/_2$ mile (excellent views of the valley) to arrive at Willy Watt Mill. Cross the stile to the lakeside and follow the directions for the shorter walk from point 3.

Great Doddington
The Stag's Head

| MAP: OS LANDRANGER 152 OR EXPLORER 224 (GR 885650) | **WALK 8** | DISTANCE: 3 MILES |

DIRECTIONS TO START: GREAT DODDINGTON LIES JUST SOUTH OF WELLINGBOROUGH AND CAN EASILY BE ACCESSED FROM THE A45 NORTHAMPTON-WELLINGBOROUGH ROAD. THE STAG'S HEAD IS ON THE MAIN ROAD AT THE EASTERN END OF THE VILLAGE. **PARKING:** AT THE STAG'S HEAD FOR PATRONS OR ON QUIET ROADSIDES IN THE VILLAGE.

High on its limestone ridge, Great Doddington looks out across the wide valley of the Nene. Along its length are a string of silvery lakes, the legacy of gravel extractors in the years of the road-building boom.

The extraction of gravel below Great Doddington began in 1989. On its completion five years later, a rather bare Summer Leys Nature Reserve was opened. Now the reeds and willows have grown and the wooden hides have weathered into the landscape. Mallards, shovellers, pintails, tufted ducks and many others inhabit the waters. This walk takes you right around the reserve (don't forget your binoculars!) and crosses the river at an old mill before returning up the hill to Great Doddington.

The Stag's Head

This started life at the end of the 17th century as a coaching inn with a smallholding. Today it is everything from a friendly local with a cosy and interesting cellar bar to a restaurant well known for its excellent Sunday lunches. And it is very used to accommodating walkers, being strategically placed on the long-distance Nene Way.

The snack menu here is promptly and interestingly served (ploughman's lunches, jackets, toasties, ham and eggs etc), but if you feel like going more up-market, you can move over to the restaurant, where an open (gas) fire greets you on cold days and two stags' heads high on the wall keep an eye on the proceedings. The home-made steak pie is said to be the most popular dish but there are plenty more to choose from – and children are welcomed with their own menu. Dogs, however, should not venture farther than the small garden.

Food is served every day from 12 noon to 2 pm and 7 pm to 9.30 pm (6.30 pm to 9 pm on Sundays) and there is a good range of accompanying wines and ales, including 6X, Black Sheep and Hook Norton. Telephone: 01933 222316.

The Walk

① From the Stag's Head, turn left along the main road. Ignore the first Nene Way signs on the left. Where the road swings right, keep straight ahead on Lower Street. There are good views across the valley to Wollaston as you go. Where Lower Street joins the main road again, follow the Nene Way signs into a little field on the left. Cross this and continue downhill across the next field. Continue down the third field and cross the stile at the bottom.

② Now turn left immediately (leaving the Nene Way) and follow the fence down to the river. Cross the little bridge and continue down the right hand side of the next two fields. Cross a plank bridge into the third field and head for a wooden bridge and steps leading to a disused railway line. Cross straight over this to an entrance into Summer Leys.

③ Turn right and keep to the obvious path around the outside of the reserve. At one point a stream enters and you are briefly taken out to a track alongside the road. Soon after this you reach picnic tables and the car park. From the car park, tarmac tracks lead out to the hides, which are generally open. When you have finished exploring, continue on the stony peripheral path along the edge of the reserve. Another hide is passed and, continuing around to the top corner, you reach a gate bringing you again onto the old railway line.

PLACES OF INTEREST NEARBY

Just a couple of miles down the road is **Earls Barton**, where the famous Saxon church attracts admirers from far and wide. To be accurate, only the tower is Saxon – the classical stone ribbing dates it fairly precisely around AD 970. And if you're impressed by this, travel a few miles north-west to **Brixworth** (west of the A508) – the church here is some 300 years older!

The Summer Leys Nature Reserve

④ Turn right and, at the tarmac road, left. Now you cross the river itself, then a lock on the navigation channel and then the mill stream. Crossing in front of the old mill, you reach a gate, through which you turn left and climb the hill. At the top left hand corner of the field, a gate takes you into the next field. Cross this directly (you can see a post in the fence) and then cross the next field in the same direction. A kissing gate now admits you to a grassy lane, which then takes you through a little field and out to the road close to the Stag's Head.

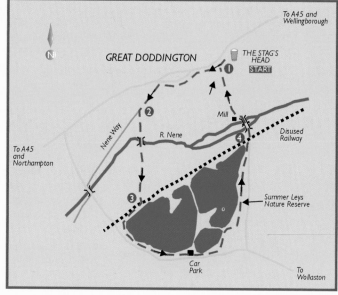

Mears Ashby
The Griffin's Head

MAP: OS LANDRANGER 152 OR EXPLORER 224 (GR 840665)

WALK 9

DISTANCE: 2½ or 4½ MILES

DIRECTIONS TO START: MEARS ASHBY IS MIDWAY BETWEEN WELLINGBOROUGH AND NORTHAMPTON. TURN NORTH OFF THE OLD ROAD (A4500), EITHER AT WILBY OR AT EARLS BARTON. THE GRIFFIN'S HEAD IS AT THE SOUTH OF THE VILLAGE. **PARKING:** AT THE GRIFFIN'S HEAD (PATRONS). TO SHORTEN YOUR WALK, YOU COULD PARK IN SYWELL COUNTRY PARK ITSELF FOR A SMALL FEE. THE DISTANCE FROM HERE (POINT 3) AROUND THE RESERVOIR IS ABOUT 2½ MILES.

A walk of just a mile across the fields from Mears Ashby will bring you to Sywell Reservoir. Created in 1903, it became redundant in the 1970s and was taken over by Northamptonshire County Council to provide the major feature of a new Country Park. Today there is an arboretum, butterfly garden, amphibian pond, play area, nature reserve – and a splendid track around the water. And if you are thinking a reservoir walk sounds rather bleak, think again! At Sywell the grassy slopes reach to the water's edge all around except for the dam. The lake is U-shaped – one arm of the U is a reedbed where wildfowl nest and dragonflies hover in summer, the other is a wooded nature reserve with hides for watching the birds. And if you need fortifying before you return to the Griffin's Head, you can always stop off at the cafeteria!

The Griffin's Head

This pub was once called 'The Boot', a common title in Northamptonshire. The more sophisticated title of Griffin's Head was taken from the coat of arms of the Stockdale family at Mears Ashby Hall. The exterior is that of a fairly imposing old house. Inside it is high-ceilinged and simply decorated, with a large bar area and cosy lounge with inglenook.

The food here is good plain fare. The basket meals are a popular choice for lunchtime snacks, but there are also all the usual ploughman's lunches, jackets, baguettes and the rest. The main menu is varied (and interestingly states 'We have attempted to make sure that all produce is GM free') and extras appear on a chalkboard. Vegetarians are well catered for.

Food is served here every lunchtime, and each evening except Sunday and Monday. Real ales include Marston's Pedigree and Wells Eagle along with guest beers – and there is always a reasonably priced 'Wine of the Month'. Telephone: 01604 812945.

The Walk

① From the Griffin's Head, walk downhill, admiring the attractive ironstone façade of Mears Ashby Hall. At the corner, take the footpath on the left, which follows the wall of the estate. At the top of the hill in the next field, follow the diagonal path cut through the crops to reach the road.

② Turn left on the road, and, in about 150 yards, take another footpath crossing a

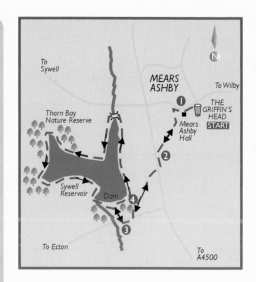

field on the right. You have fine views of Sywell Reservoir as you go. The path maintains the same direction across a second field to reach another road beside a red brick house. The entrance to Sywell Country Park is about 100 yards along on the right.

③ Once in the park, there is plenty to see – fine trees, the amphibian pond, butterfly garden and more. Reserve them for your return, and walk ahead towards the steps leading up the dam to the reservoir. Just before the steps, a track on the right climbs rather more gently to the water's edge.

④ And now there is no more need for directions – just follow the path around the water's edge in an anti-clockwise direction. When you reach the top of the first arm of the U, a wooden causeway will take you across the reeds and bulrushes around one of the feeder streams. After more grassland with clumps of silver birch, you reach the nature reserve with

Sywell Reservoir

its thickets of alder, hawthorn and blackthorn. Here a second stream enters the reservoir and you can make your way to the hide at the water's edge. Leaving the reserve, a good hard-surfaced track (suitable for wheelchairs and pushchairs) takes you back to the dam.

Take a few moments to look around before leaving the park and retracing your steps to Mears Ashby. The trees are particularly interesting – planted originally by the Water Board, you can identify giant redwood, Wellingtonia, Monterey pine and others. A leaflet from the information office will help. And as you leave, take a glance at the old sheepwash to the right of the exit – local farmers used this site for over 200 years to prepare sheep for shearing.

> ### PLACES OF INTEREST NEARBY
> For a total contrast to the peace of the country park, go along to **Billing Aquadrome**, 4 miles away on the outskirts of Northampton. Children will love this riverside site with its funfair, mini-train, boating lake and swimming pool. Telephone: 01604 408181.

33

Yardley Hastings
The Rose and Crown

DIRECTIONS TO START: YARDLEY HASTINGS LIES JUST NORTH OF THE A428 NORTHAMPTON-BEDFORD ROAD, 7 MILES EAST OF NORTHAMPTON. FROM THAT ROAD, TAKE THE WESTERN TURNING INTO THE VILLAGE (IE THE ONE NEAREST NORTHAMPTON) TO FIND THE ROSE AND CROWN. **PARKING:** AT THE ROSE AND CROWN FOR PATRONS OR ON QUIET ROADSIDES IN THE VILLAGE.

The pretty stone village of Yardley Hastings is on the edge of the Castle Ashby estate – an ideal spot to embark on a walk around this splendid house and parkland.

Castle Ashby is one of Northamptonshire's jewels – an Elizabethan mansion set above lawns sweeping down to lakes in the valley. The parkland is recognisably the work of Capability Brown. The house was built in the late 16th century by the Compton family who became the Earls of Northampton. Although the house is not open to visitors, this walk will give you a good view of it from all sides – and you can always take time out for a stroll around the beautiful gardens.

The Rose and Crown

This pleasant little village pub is a place of indeterminate age – the original is possibly 15th century, but there have been many additions and alterations since. The result is an establishment on various levels from the bar at the bottom (papered in currency notes from around the world) to the eating areas in steps above. Flag floors and low-beamed ceilings complete the scene.

The Rose and Crown is establishing a reputation for its attractively-presented and extensive menu. Most popular is the carvery, which does not confine itself to Sundays but is on offer five days of the week (not Monday or Wednesday). But if it's just a simple snack you have in mind, there are sandwiches, soups and ploughman's lunches (if you can resist the rest) – and the delicious-looking desserts are all home made. Food is served here from 12 noon to 2 pm and 7 pm to 9.30 pm every day. Children are welcomed and appropriate portions are served. Dogs, however, must remain outside. The draught beers served in this free house are Adnams, Wadworth 6X and Greene King Abbot. Telephone: 01604 696276.

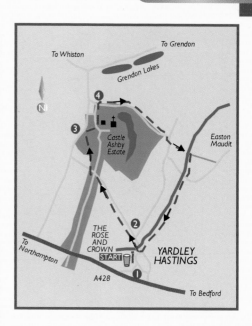

The Walk

① Leaving the Rose and Crown, walk downhill towards the centre of the village. At the square, bear left and continue past the school. Where the road swings right, go straight ahead (past the grass triangle) and walk down Little Lane beside the brook. At the bridge, cross over the brook and walk through the woodland to the next bridge. Now turn left on the road and continue to the junction with the Grendon road.

② Keep straight ahead here – the road is quiet and there are grassy banks. After about 15 minutes walking, you arrive at the long (2 miles, in fact!) avenue of Castle Ashby House. Crossing over, you have the house on your right and the woodland of Yardley Chase on your left. Just on the far side, take the footpath across the field on the right (go straight ahead and turn right at the road junction if you prefer tarmac). The footpath goes slightly diagonally to a stile that admits you to the parkland of the House. Maintain the same direction across it to reach the road at the far corner.

③ Turn right immediately on an earth path under the trees. This takes you through the grounds to the front of Castle

Castle Ashby House seen through the trees

Ashby House (turn right for the gardens). Now bear left and walk down the path beside the grassy car park. At the road, keep straight ahead beside the wall to reach the tiny village green with its horse chestnuts.

④ Turn right and follow the narrow road right through the estate – there are views of Grendon Lakes ahead and, at the top of the hill, views of the private lakes in the grounds. On reaching the road junction, turn right. This road will take you right back to Yardley Hastings (1 mile), but there is a prettier alternative. About 150 yards along, take the footpath descending

PLACES OF INTEREST NEARBY

Although **Castle Ashby House** is not open to the public, you can get a good view of it from the main gates. The gardens are open every day of the year and are well worth a visit. Near the entrance, the 'Farmyard' houses an assortment of craft and antique shops and an interesting restaurant. Telephone: 01604 696696.

across the field on the left. Cross the stream, and then turn right and follow beside it all the way back to Yardley Hastings. You arrive at the bridge you crossed at the outset, and can retrace your steps to the Rose and Crown.

Stoke Bruerne
The Boat Inn

MAP: OS LANDRANGER 152 OR EXPLORER 207 (GR 743499)

WALK 11

DISTANCE: 3½ MILES

DIRECTIONS TO START: STOKE BRUERNE IS 6 MILES SOUTH OF NORTHAMPTON, JUST WEST OF THE A508. THE BOAT INN IS BESIDE THE CANAL. **PARKING:** THERE IS LIMITED PARKING AT THE BOAT INN FOR PATRONS. ON THE OPPOSITE SIDE OF THE CANAL, A PUBLIC CAR PARK FOR THE WHARF CHARGES A SMALL FEE. ROADSIDE PARKING IS PROHIBITED IN THE VILLAGE.

Stoke Bruerne has been described as 'the best example of a canalside village in this country'. Seven locks carry the Grand Union Canal (see also Walk 12) up to the busy wharf, where, along with the pub, there is an award-winning Canal Museum and shop, an old boat weighing machine and a trip boat, the *Indian Chief*. Further on the canal plunges into Blisworth tunnel, where in pre-steam days, the boats were taken through by 'leggers' walking on the walls. The horse walked over the top – and it is on the horse path that this walk sets out.

There is plenty to see on this pleasant ramble – the little village of Shutlanger with its 'monastery', the headwaters of the River Tove, and the architecturally famous Stoke Park Pavilions. But reserve a little time at the end of the day to sit under the poplar trees beside the wharf and take in the excitements of boating life at Stoke Bruerne.

The Boat Inn

This large thatched building stands alongside the wharf. Inside you can eat in the canalside bar, tap room, bistro, lounge bar or restaurant – choose the ambience to suit your mood! The tap room and canalside bar are part of the original old pub, tiny bare rooms overlooking the canal, and heated by open coal fires in winter. The pleasant lounge with its half-boat bar is at the back of the building. Here a circular stone chimney houses the fire – electric! – while the nautical effect is provided by high 'clinker-built' wooden ceilings with brass lamps. The bar menu is excellent with everything from home-made soup to fried seafood platter. Most popular is said to be the 'flooded butty' – a baguette filled with chips, swamped with onion and mushroom gravy and topped with cheese! Ales served include Marston's Pedigree and John Smith's Bitter. Children are welcomed in the lounge bar, while the same courtesy is extended to dogs in the tap room and canalside bar.

To get the best view of the canal you will have to spend a little more and eat in the first floor restaurant. The likes of braised Barbary duck with port and peppercorn sauce might convince you it's worthwhile! Food is served at the Boat every lunchtime (12 noon to 2 pm) and evening (from about 6 pm), although the restaurant is not open on Mondays. In the height of the summer meals are available throughout the day at this very popular pub – but it might be worth reserving your table. Telephone: 01604 862428.

The Walk

① From the Boat, cross over the lock (or the bridge) and walk along the towpath, passing the museum. Carry on beside the line of boats until you see the tunnel mouth ahead. Now take a broad obvious track leading uphill – the one-time horses' path. After a few minutes you find a footpath signed across a field on the left (just before the remains of a bridge). The footpath takes you to the right of a big farm to reach the road.

② Cross over to the footpath opposite. At the bottom of the hill, bear left and follow beside the hedge of a long field. At its end you are signed across two more fields to reach the road. Turn right to arrive at the crossroads in Shutlanger.

③ Turn left down Water Lane (the building on the left is called The Monastery – although it probably never was one). At its end, continue across the field in the direction of a farm on the hill opposite. Reaching a metal gate before a farm track, cross the brook and turn left. Now you have a pleasant stretch (perhaps 20 minutes) alongside the brook, as it hurries to join the River Tove. The stream gathers strength as you go, and finally heads off into fields on the left. Your path

PLACES OF INTEREST NEARBY

You need go no farther than Stoke Bruerne! The **Canal Museum** is the best of its kind and is open every day except Mondays in winter. The *Indian Chief* takes visitors on the short trip to the tunnel mouth in summer and at weekends. For details of both, telephone: 01604 862229. **Stoke Park Pavilions** are the work of Inigo Jones and are open to the public at weekends in July and August.

Approaching Blisworth Tunnel

ahead is obvious (there is now a ditch beside you) and you pass through a couple of gates before reaching another footpath on the left (if you get to a big bridge across the river you have gone too far).

④ Turn left and follow this footpath uphill across fields. It emerges at the drive to Stoke Park Pavilions. Your route continues ahead and almost immediately crosses a stile into a field on the left. Now walk downhill heading for the line of poplars (they once lined the drive to Stoke Park House). Beyond them a gate takes you to a grassy lane. Follow this now to Stoke Bruerne, passing a nature reserve on the site of an old brickworks on your right. The track finally curves to meet the road – the Boat is just to your left.

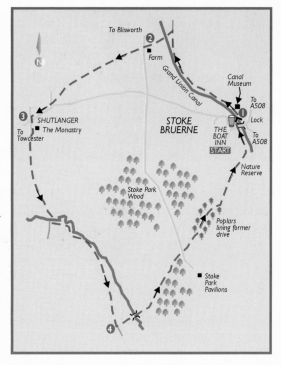

Cosgrove
The Navigation Inn

MAP: OS LANDRANGER 152 OR EXPLORER 207 (GR 788436)

WALK 12

DISTANCE: 2 MILES

DIRECTIONS TO START: COSGROVE LIES JUST NORTH-WEST OF MILTON KEYNES. THE NAVIGATION INN IS MOST EASILY ACCESSED BY TURNING EAST OFF THE A508. AFTER ABOUT 300 YARDS, TAKE A LEFT TURN (SIGNPOSTED TO CASTLETHORPE). THE NAVIGATION IS ON THE LEFT BEFORE THE CANAL.
PARKING: AT THE NAVIGATION INN FOR PATRONS. ALTERNATIVELY, PARK IN COSGOVE AND START THE WALK FROM POINT 2.

The Grand Union Canal is the M1 of the inland waterways system – the fastest and most direct link between London and Birmingham. As with its motorway counterpart, the construction was not without its difficulties and controversies. Just south of Cosgrove, the 'Iron Trunk' aqueduct across the Great Ouse proved to be one of the most demanding feats of engineering, while Cosgrove itself had its main street cut in half by the new canal. Cosgrove Lodge agreed to the canal across its parkland on condition that the bridge was built in Gothic style to match its own architecture.

All these features can be seen on your walk – and though coal barges no longer ply the waters, the Grand Union remains the busiest of canals. You are sure to meet colourful narrowboats whatever the time of year as you stroll along its banks.

The Navigation Inn

This inn comes into its own on a bright summer's day when you can sit in the garden – or, even better, on the terrace – and enjoy your meal looking out over all the activity of the canal. The pub has always been popular with boaters and there should be plenty of comings and goings for entertainment. The building itself was thought to have been originally a warehouse alongside the new canal, but its role must soon have changed as there has certainly been a hostelry here for almost 200 years.

The Navigation serves meals every lunchtime and evening in its wood-panelled restaurant and bar – and even if you can't sit outside, you can still enjoy a view of the canal and, in winter, a blazing log fire in a huge brick fireplace. The food is fairly standard – lasagne, scampi, chicken, steaks – but you can rise to smoked salmon or go Mexican with fajitas. The desserts are perhaps more original – bread and butter pudding made with home-baked bread, and baked Alaska cooked to order, as well as daily specials. All dishes are attractively and very promptly served. For lighter lunches, sandwiches, baguettes and ploughman's are on offer. Beverages include Greene King IPA and Abbot Ale and the popular Morland Old Speckled Hen. Children are welcomed everywhere except the bar – but dogs should definitely confine themselves to the garden. Telephone: 01908 543156.

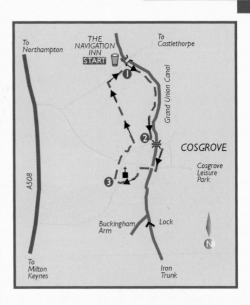

The Walk

① Cross the road from the Navigation, and without crossing the canal, take the path downhill to join the towpath. Now you have about half an hour's stroll beside the lively tree-fringed canal. Over to your left (across the canal) is the valley of the River Tove, here the boundary with Buckinghamshire. From here the land sweeps up to the horizon crowned by the steep spire of Hanslope church, looking out over Buckinghamshire, Bedfordshire and Northamptonshire. The canal curves around to the village of Cosgrove and arrives at the honey-stone carved Gothic bridge.

② Walk up to the road, cross the bridge and descend to the towpath on the opposite side. Now you are at the old Cosgrove Wharf. If you have time and would like a longer walk, continue ahead, passing Cosgrove Lock and the marina on the site of the old Buckingham Arm. A further 15 minutes or so walking will bring

Cosgrove's Gothic bridge

you to the aqueduct over the Ouse, the 'Iron Trunk'. But to continue with this short stroll, turn left down some steps to the road below (the old main street) and double back through the tunnel under the canal. Now take a gravelled road on the left, just before the Barley Mow (a pub with a reputation for real ales). From this, a tarmacked track leads off on the right at the back of the houses. The path takes you into the churchyard and around the old church (well worth a look – especially the 15th century timbered roof). The path comes out to the road.

③ Turn right on the road, continue ahead at the road junction, and then, just as the road bends right to the bridge, take a bridleway on the left between the houses.

The bridleway runs along the backs of some gardens, and then continues across the tops of three fields (keep the hedge immediately on your left). It is well signed and well trodden, and there are easy gates between the fields. On reaching the road, turn right to return to the Navigation.

PLACES OF INTEREST NEARBY

Cosgrove Leisure Park, on the site of the now-demolished Cosgrove Lodge, offers swimming, tennis, picnic and play areas, fishing, shops and a restaurant for a small entrance fee. The **Ouse Valley Park** is an attractive nature conservation area beside the Great Ouse. From the Iron Trunk, walk down to the valley below and follow the marked track.

Eastcote
The Eastcote Arms

| MAP: OS LANDRANGER 152 OR EXPLORER 207 (GR 680539) | **WALK 13** | DISTANCE: $2^1/_2$ MILES |

DIRECTIONS TO START: FROM THE A5 AT FOSTER'S BOOTH, $3^1/_2$ MILES NORTH OF TOWCESTER, TURN OFF TO THE NORTH-EAST. THEN GO RIGHT AND LEFT, FOLLOWING SIGNS TO EASTCOTE. FINALLY TURN RIGHT DOWN THE VILLAGE STREET TO FIND THE EASTCOTE ARMS. **PARKING:** AT THE EASTCOTE ARMS FOR PATRONS, OTHERWISE ROADSIDE IN THE VILLAGE.

Eastcote is one of the five villages (Foster's Booth, Pattishall, Astcote, Eastcote and Dalscote) collectively referred to as Pattishall. They are old villages, set in a rolling green landscape and grouped around the valley of a little stream heading north to join the Nene. In the last century they played their part in the thriving shoe industry of Northampton.

On this walk you will pass many reminders of former times as you follow the paths that were once so important to the villagers. At Astcote, the former red brick shoe factory still stands beside the green, the tower of Pattishall church shows Saxon brickwork and a house in Eastcote has a mounting block and tethering ring beside its door for horse riders long-gone.

The Eastcote Arms

This friendly, traditional and very old village pub has a reputation for good food and ale. The building itself dates from the beginning of the 17th century – beside a horn on the wall, an inscription tells you that Cromwell's men roasted an ox and played 'loop the horn' here on their way to the Battle of Naseby in the summer of 1645. The interior with its low beams, coathooks on the bar and tiny eating rooms is functional as it must always have been, but nevertheless the place oozes atmosphere.

Food is served at the Eastcote Arms every lunchtime except Monday, and on Thursday, Friday and Saturday evenings. Sunday lunch is a popular event. The midday menu of sandwiches, baguettes, ploughman's lunches and jackets is fairly standard, but always additionally includes home-made soup and a chef's special such as steak and ale pie or baked sausage casserole (highly recommended!). The evening choice is wider, extending to 'Rita Craddock's mixed grill', poached salmon and vegetarian dishes, among others. Accompanying beverages include Bateman's Best Bitter, Greene King Abbot Ale and guest beers. Children are very welcome; dogs however, must content themselves with the small but pleasant garden beside the car park. Telephone: 01327 830731.

The Walk

① Leaving the Eastcote Arms car park, turn right down the village street. Passing an old stone barn, notice the antlers high

PLACES OF INTEREST NEARBY

A couple of miles to the north-west is the **Old Dairy Farm Centre** at Upper Stowe. Here children can make the acquaintance of the farm animals while their parents can indulge in a little retail therapy in the fascinating shops of the Craft Centre. A restaurant caters for all. Telephone: 01327 340525.

on its wall! On the right at the end of the village is a house called The Old Boot – it was obviously once a pub. Beside the house a fingerpost directs you into the field. Now bear diagonally left to descend to the stream at the bottom of the slope and the handsome wooden bridge that crosses it. Maintain the same direction and climb the field, heading for a gap to the right of the red barn. Continue across the next field to its corner beside the house – the bottom of the field is often boggy (notice the marsh plants here) but you can skirt it.

② Turn left into Astcote. At the village green (the old shoe factory faces you), take a path on the right going between houses and across the front of another house. Bear right around a hedge of Leylandii, and continue across a field and down a narrow track. At its end, go through a gate on the left. The cross-field path now bears right to a stile in the hedge, after which you cut off (or walk around) the corner of the next field and then turn right. The path now heads uphill with the hedge on your right. Keep to it over the hill and down to reach the road in Pattishall.

③ Cross straight over and follow the alleyway up and to the right to reach a

The path back to Eastcote

road. Turn left to the pretty village green with its little shop, and then right past a large thatched house. Ahead is the church – take a few moments to look around. Continue down the road to the crossroads at the bottom of the hill.

④ Cross straight over and continue until you see a footpath signed across the field on the left (this field was the site of a First World War naval prisoner of war camp – the prisoners constructed a model harbour on the brook). This footpath comes out to a road, which you cross to another footpath opposite. Now descend the slope to another wooden bridge and climb uphill again. At the top of the field, bear to the right

to reach a tarmacked road. Turn left, passing Barton Mead, the house with a mounting block beside the door and a ring in the wall. Turn left to return to the Eastcote Arms.

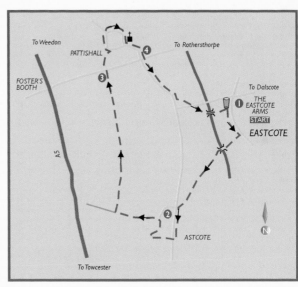

Abthorpe
The New Inn

MAP: OS LANDRANGER 152 OR EXPLORER 207 (GR 649465)	**WALK 14**	**DISTANCE:** 2 MILES

DIRECTIONS TO START: ABTHORPE LIES 3 MILES SOUTH-WEST OF TOWCESTER. IT CAN BE REACHED FROM TOWCESTER ON AN UNCLASSIFIED ROAD OR FROM THE A43 VIA SILVERSTONE. THE NEW INN IS WELL CONCEALED IN A CUL-DE-SAC BEHIND THE VILLAGE GREEN AND CHURCH. **PARKING:** THE NEW INN HAS LIMITED PARKING FOR PATRONS ONLY. OTHERWISE, FIND A QUIET ROADSIDE IN THE VILLAGE.

On the banks of the infant River Tove, Abthorpe is undoubtedly one of Northamptonshire's prettiest – and least known – villages. A plaque on the immaculate village green before the church tells you that on numerous occasions it has been the winner of the 'Best-kept village' award. At the far end of the green, the old stone school has long lost its children but still proudly displays its bell. And after you have taken this walk you are sure to agree that Abthorpe has a greater concentration of footpaths than anywhere else in the county!

This particular route takes you over the Tove to neighbouring Slapton. The tiny village boasts thatched cottages, an old manor, a restored mill beside the river and an attractive mellow stone church set apart in a meadow. From here a path climbs the hill for a long look down the length of the river valley and beyond before returning to Abthorpe.

The New Inn

This inn is new only in name – the building is in fact an amalgamation of two small one-time thatched cottages of unknown vintage. During the summer, bright hanging baskets offset the old grey stone most attractively. In the tiny rear garden, pots of all shapes and sizes spill over with riotous colour, creating a very pleasant corner for an alfresco meal on warm days. Should you be here when the weather is not so welcoming, the interior is cosy and comfortable with dining areas on various levels. An inglenook, low beams and horse-brasses complete the picture.

The menu here is not extensive, but the pub is included because it is a homely family-run business – the friendly and helpful owners were happy to make up a very good ploughman's although it did not appear on the menu. Snacks that do appear are sandwiches, baguettes and jackets, but for more substantial meals (evenings only), you could enjoy steak, fish, grills, lasagne and vegetarian dishes. Food is served every lunchtime (12.15 pm onwards) and evening (6.30 pm onwards) except Monday and children and dogs are both welcome – the latter confined to the bar area. A good range of beers and ales is on offer to complement the meal. Telephone: 01327 857306.

The Walk

① Coming out from the short road to the New Inn, turn left down the lane. At its end, a stile takes you into a field, where you bear over to the left to find another stile in the hedge. Bear right in the next field and in the third field cross the embankment of a former railway to an attractive wooden bridge arching over the river. The path ahead takes you to the gates of Slapton Mill. Several footpaths head off on the left, but ignore them and walk through the gates and up the lane into the village.

② Reaching the village street, turn left. Pass a variety of interesting properties before turning right up Church Lane. Now to find the church! At the end of the lane, turn left on a path beside the long wall of a house. This leads you out to a tarmacked track into a field – and there to the right is the low squat little church. You can get the key if you want to explore. But to continue, turn left now and walk down to the road again. Turn right passing old stone Slapton Lodge and continue over river and railway to meet the main road.

③ Follow the road to the left (with care) for about 300 yards, past Highfield Farm to a telegraph pole and pub sign on the right. Behind these a gate admits you to a bridleway climbing the hill. Keep the hedge first on your right and then on your

Abthorpe

left, passing a pond. With a field ahead, turn left through a gate onto a broad track. This climbs to the top of the hill and there are good views along the valley of the Tove. Slapton and Abthorpe are below you, and over to the left, the tower of Wappenham church stands out from the hillside. Keep to this

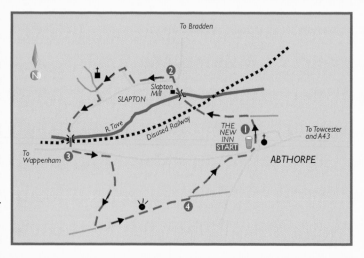

farm track until you are quite close to the first houses of Abthorpe.

④ Now take the inviting path heading off across a field on the left in the direction of Abthorpe church and then descending to the road. Turn right along the raised 'pavement' and then left down Main Street to return to the start.

Weston
The Crown Inn

MAP: OS LANDRANGER 152 OR EXPLORER 207 (GR 589469)	**WALK 15**	DISTANCE: $3\frac{1}{4}$ MILES (WITH A POSSIBLE SHORT CUT)

DIRECTIONS TO START: WESTON IS ABOUT 6 MILES NORTH OF BRACKLEY AND CAN BE REACHED FROM THE B4525 ON A MINOR ROAD THROUGH HELMDON. THE CROWN IS AT THE ROAD JUNCTION IN THE VILLAGE. **PARKING:** AT THE CROWN FOR PATRONS OR ON QUIET ROADSIDES IN THE VILLAGE.

In the most rural part of Northamptonshire, the twin villages of Weston and Weedon Lois overlook the upper valley of the River Tove. The walk begins in the attractive village of Weston. Imposing Weston Hall has for many years been in the possession of the Sitwell family, well known for their literary talents. Opposite the Hall is another noteworthy residence, dating from 1588 and named, aptly enough, Armada House. The way leads on to Weedon Lois, where a few grassy humps in a field are all that remain of an old priory – except for the fishponds, which are now the domain of the local angling club! The village church gazes down on the peaceful scene.

The Crown Inn

All Souls' College in Oxford was the first recorded owner of the Crown, way back in the time of Elizabeth I. The pub was once a coaching inn, the present day function room being the old coach house. The Crown has retained its character to this day, and is a genuine local with low ceilings, beams, quarry-tiled floor, roaring log fires in winter and high-backed settles. Décor is simple – a few harnesses and horseshoes deck the bare walls – but the friendly landlord does offer you something to meditate on as you dine. His quote for the day is chalked on a board in the lounge area!

The menu here is not extensive, although the usual sandwiches and baguettes are available as well as vegetarian dishes and a children's platter. There are interesting and excellent 'specials' too – try organic lamb, perhaps, or free-range chicken with apples, mushrooms, brandy and cream. To accompany the meal there is a good range of ales including Wadworth 6X, Ruddles Smooth and Marston's Pedigree. The Crown serves food every evening from 6.30 pm to 9 pm and on Friday, Saturday and Sunday lunchtimes from 12 noon to 2 pm. There are a few tables outside for a sunny day. Telephone: 01295 760310.

The Walk

① Leaving the Crown, turn right along the main street. Where the road swings left, Weston Hall is on your left. Turn right here beside the green (overlooked by Armada House) and at the end of the

PLACES OF INTEREST NEARBY

Sulgrave Manor, 3 miles south-west of Weston, was the ancestral home of the Washington family and as such attracts a good number of transatlantic visitors. Guided tours, gardens, refreshments and occasional 'events' (be prepared to find yourself in the American Civil War, for example) make this a popular venue. Telephone: 01295 760205.

cul-de-sac continue on the footpath. This soon reaches a field, and immediately turns right to cross the stream. On the far side, a fence first confines the path to the field edge (if overgrown, continue on the opposite side of the brook instead). Eventually the path runs through open fields, still closely following the wooded banks of the brook.

② On passing through a gate and reaching a hard-surfaced track, you have a choice. To the left the track leads up to Weedon Lois directly. If you are here in the winter when the fields are ploughed or muddy it may be advisable to go that way. When you reach the road in the village, turn right to view the church, the Sitwell memorial and the fishponds. In summer, it is pleasant to continue ahead beside the clear brook through the green meadow. After 15 minutes or so walking, the track leaves the brook to head uphill.

③ Now find a stile in the hedge on the left. On the far side turn left and immediately cross the brook on a plank bridge hidden in the trees. Again turn left and follow the opposite bank for about 50 yards.

④ Take a path on the right, crossing the field. Several more fields are then crossed

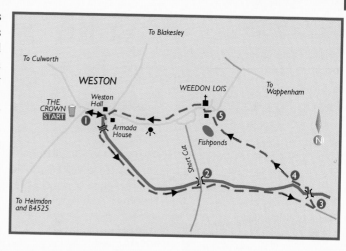

as the path climbs towards Weedon Lois – the route is well marked and, in summer, cut clearly through the crops. The last, steeply sloping field is Church Close where the priory once stood – to the left are the fishponds. Cross the field towards a stile just left of the thatched cottage. A path leads to the road.

⑤ Turn left to reach the church. Opposite is the churchyard extension, where Dame Edith Sitwell's memorial looks out across the valley. When ready, continue beside the road to return to Weston. The path is pleasantly set back from the carriageway and there are good views all the way.

The clear path through the fields

Aynho
The Cartwright Arms

| **MAP:** OS LANDRANGER 151 OR EXPLORER 191 (GR 515332) | **WALK 16** | **DISTANCE:** $3^1/_2$ MILES |

DIRECTIONS TO START: AYNHO IS 5 MILES SOUTH-EAST OF BANBURY. THE CARTWRIGHT ARMS IS ON THE MAIN ROAD THROUGH THE VILLAGE, THE B4031. **PARKING:** AT THE CARTWRIGHT ARMS FOR PATRONS ONLY. OTHERWISE ON QUIET ROADSIDES IN THE VILLAGE.

At the southernmost tip of North-amptonshire, Aynho seems more a part of the Cotswolds with its lovely honey-stone thatched dwellings. But the cottages of Aynho have a hallmark of their own – their walls are clothed with apricot trees. Aynho has been dubbed the 'Apricot Village'. It seems that at one time the squire here accepted apricots in part payment for rent!

The walk from Aynho takes you through fields and woods and across the Ockley Brook, here the boundary with Oxford-shire. On the far side you reach the equally attractive village of Souldern with its squat grey church and pretty village pond. Heading for home, the path then skirts the grounds of Aynho Park, once the seat of the Cartwright family but now converted to private dwellings. The first building here was burned to the ground by Royalist troops retreating from the Battle of Naseby. Charles II later paid compensation for this destruction and the present edifice dates from that time.

The Cartwright Arms

Once upon a time this part of North-amptonshire was known as 'Cart-wright's Corner'. The Cartwright family were extensive landowners here for over 300 years, and you will find references to various members of the family in the village. Sadly the last squire and his heir were killed in a car accident in 1954 and the line is no more. The Cartwright Arms is in fact a hotel and has been offering accommodation since the coaching days of the 16th century. The cobbles under the archway have survived from that day.

Meals for both residents and visitors are taken in the informal setting of the lounge bar, where beams, horse-brasses and a log-burning stove (in winter) give a cosy feel. Children are welcomed here and there is even a corner for dogs. A few outside tables are also provided for sunny days. The menu is quite wide – pork fillet in a creamed brandy sauce sounds exciting, but there are also the usual steaks, pies, curries and a selection of vegetarian dishes. The food is promptly and pleasantly served and the range of beverages includes Ruddles Best, Guinness and Scrumpy Jack. Lunchtime and evening meals are served every day. Telephone: 01869 811110.

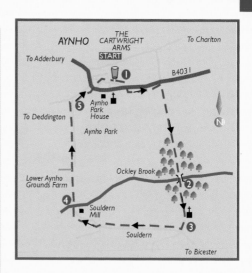

The Walk

① Leaving the Cartwright Arms, turn left and follow the main road (passing the Jacobean Old Grammar School) to the end of the village. Reaching the Portway, cross the road and take the footpath between two walls on the opposite side.

This eventually reaches open fields. Continue beside a fence on the right to a wood. Two white discs now point the way across the next field, after which a gate on the left opens on to a concrete track. Follow the track down through the woodland to cross the stream – you are now in Oxfordshire.

② Continue ahead. Reaching a field, keep first to the fence, then aim for a stile to the left of a row of tall conifers. A track beside the stream leads to a concrete track passing the church.

③ Reaching the road beside the pond, turn right and walk through the picturesque village. At the far end, where the road swings left, continue ahead on the concrete track to cross the brook at Souldern Mill.

④ Now carry on uphill on the concrete track. Soon the narrow road from Lower Aynho Grounds Farm joins you on the left and you continue ahead with the wall of Aynho Park on your right.

Aynho Park House

⑤ Turn right and walk beside the park wall uphill to Aynho. At the road junction, cross over to Little Lane, almost opposite. This brings you up to The Square with its interesting old houses. One has a yew tree growing out of the garden wall. A lane on the right leads back to the Cartwright Arms. But if you have a few moments to spare, turn left to look at the old houses of Blacksmith's Hill or walk a short way along the main road to view the façade of Aynho Park.

PLACES OF INTEREST NEARBY

Four miles north is **King's Sutton**, where the church with its splendid spire overlooks a village green ringed with houses dating from the 16th century. On the Charlton road, is **St Rumbold's Well**, where the waters were once said to cure disorders of the stomach, liver, spleen, kidneys, heart, brain, nerves and muscles! The NCC has recently added a plaque 'Water unfit for drinking'!

Chacombe
The George and Dragon

DIRECTIONS TO START: CHACOMBE LIES JUST NORTH-EAST OF BANBURY, BETWEEN THE A361 AND THE B4525. THE GEORGE AND DRAGON IS AT THE WEST END OF THE VILLAGE – IF COMING FROM THE A361, TAKE THE FIRST ROAD ON THE LEFT. **PARKING:** AT THE GEORGE AND DRAGON FOR PATRONS OR ON QUIET ROADSIDES IN THE VILLAGE.

The little village of Chacombe hides in a wooded valley between the rolling hills. This attractive area is Northamptonshire's 'wolds', an easterly extension of the Cotswolds. The stone here is perhaps a shade darker, but the villages are just as pretty. Over the hill from Chacombe lies the larger village of Middleton Cheney with its splendidly spired 14th century church. The windows are by William Morris and are said to be one of the finest collections of 19th century stained glass in the country – it's worth getting the key to take a look. The route home climbs yet another gentle hill and offers fine distant views across the valley of the River Cherwell.

The George and Dragon

This glowing honey-stone building dates from the 16th century. At its rear is a recent extension, which, once inside, you feel is even older than the original! Some parts of it certainly are – the warped wooden door was once that of a church and the twisted beams are salvaged from an old barn. Bare floors, high-backed settles and wintertime log fires complete the picture – and through the stone archway are yet two more comfortable bars in the old part of the building. If you absolutely must sit outside, there are a few tables on the edge of the parking area.

Chalked on a huge blackboard, the menu here is wide reaching, with particularly interesting fish dishes – the humblest is mixed fish in a caraway seed cream, but you could upgrade to orange tilapia fish with mushroom couscous! If you can resist this sort of temptation, there is still plenty in the snack line, with sandwiches, baguettes and filled jackets. The range of beers and real ales is similarly extensive, and includes Theakston Best, Theakston XB and Courage Directors. Food is served every day both at lunchtime and in the evening and the pub itself is open from noon to 11 pm. Children and dogs are welcomed. Telephone: 01295 711500.

The Walk

① From the pub, walk up Thorpe Road through the village. At the road junction, turn left and continue on this road out of the village, passing the school. Take the second footpath on the right – soon after

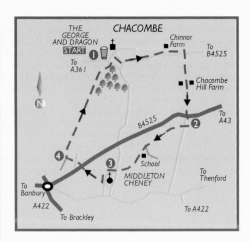

passing Chinnor Farm on the left. This grassy track climbs the hill to a farm, from where you descend on the drive to reach the main road.

② Take the road directly opposite. About 200 yards along, follow a footpath on the right leading up beside the hedge. This path cuts across the corner of a second field to reach the school at the top of the hill. Go through the gate to the right of the school and continue on the track to the main road.

③ Cross over to Glover's Lane opposite. Follow the lane where it bends left around the church wall and continue past the church. Now find a grassy lane on the right, just after the shop. At its top corner, a narrow path leads down to a stile. You are now on the Jurassic Way, a long-distance path, and can follow the shell markers. These take you down over the brook, then uphill to the road. Cross straight over and then cross the next field in the same direction. Continue over a tarmacked track and across another field.

④ At the top hedge, turn right and follow

The former priory at Chacombe can be seen across the fields

the track, which descends through a gate. Gnarled and twisted ash trees now line the path. Eventually you reach an open field. Head for some conifers on the skyline and go through an iron kissing gate concealed on the edge of the wood. A sunken path now leads out to follow the edge of the wood with some distant views. The house below and to the left was once an Augustinian priory and was rebuilt shortly after Henry VIII's dissolution. At a stile, turn away from the wood, downhill across a field, to a stile at its bottom right-hand corner beside some old sheep sheds. The shell signs now lead out through a

PLACES OF INTEREST NEARBY

The stained glass windows at **Middleton Cheney** are quite special – an address to collect the key is posted in the church porch. William Buckley, rector here in the latter half of the 19th century, was a friend of Edward Burne-Jones – who then designed the chancel windows in his memory. Many others are by William Morris. A leaflet in the church will take you on tour.

copse of yew trees to emerge on the road in Chacombe. Briefly turn left, and then right to return to the George and Dragon.

Upper Boddington
The Plough Inn

MAP: OS LANDRANGER 151 OR EXPLORER 206 (GR 485534)

WALK 18

DISTANCE: 2½ MILES; RESERVOIR CIRCUIT 1½ MILES

DIRECTIONS TO START: FROM THE A361 DAVENTRY-BANBURY ROAD, TURN WEST AT BYFIELD (SIGNPOSTED TO UPPER BODDINGTON). PASS FIRST THE CAR PARK, THEN THE RESERVOIR ON YOUR LEFT. TO REACH THE PLOUGH INN CONTINUE ON THE ROAD TO THE TOP OF THE HILL. **PARKING:** THERE IS NO CAR PARK AT THE PLOUGH INN – PARK ON QUIET ROADSIDES IN THE VILLAGE. FOR JUST THE RESERVOIR CIRCUIT, PARK IN THE CAR PARK EAST OF THE RESERVOIR AND START AT POINT 2.

Boddington was the last of three reservoirs built some 200 years ago to feed the ever-thirsty summit of the South Oxford Canal. The first of the reservoirs, Byfield, is now the Byfield Pool Nature Reserve, well known for its wealth of wildfowl. The walk passes by its edge, but you can take a detour for a closer look. Boddington Reservoir, still in use and managed by British Waterways, is a quiet and peaceful stretch of water in a rolling landscape of patchwork fields. The path around its shores is very pleasant, with woods on the east side and open fields on the west. Banbury Sailing Club is based here and the bright sails bobbing on a summer's day add to the attractive scene. For a short stroll, you could simply circuit the reservoir – but for added interest, start from the fascinating Plough Inn in the village of Upper Boddington and return across the fields.

The Plough Inn

This highly individual inn is quite unique in Northamptonshire The building is a thatched cottage dating from around 1550 and inside are two rooms, one a bar area, the other a tiny dining room known as 'Doll's Parlour'. The bar is low-beamed and bare-floored, its walls pasted with old paper cuttings from around the world. At one end are the darts and skittles, at the other a huge fire, lit throughout the year on any day with a chill in the air. Doll's Parlour takes you back to the 1930s or thereabouts. Here are the piano and aspidistra, phonograph, toby jugs, family portraits and all the rest, the owner's personal collection. The dining tables are squeezed in between.

The food in this unusual pub is first-class, with a good selection of vegetarian fare and surprisingly some Indian dishes. But for a real lunchtime treat, try a ham sandwich! This delicious thick-sliced ham has been home cooked in beer and the accompanying salad leaves more sophisticated establishments in the shade. Furthermore, there will be no hole in the pocket! A good range of beers including Castlemaine XXX and Tetley Bitter is on offer to complement the meal. Children are very welcome at the Plough, but dogs should be a little cautious as the proprietor's own are usually behind the bar. There are a few outside tables for fine days. Food is served every day except Sunday. Telephone: 01327 260364.

The Walk

① Leave the Plough and walk downhill on the road in the direction of Byfield. After about $1/2$ mile you reach a small car park on the right and, through it, steps leading up onto the dam. At the end of the dam, continue across the red brick bridge and take the path behind the trees. This brings you to the reservoir's main car park, where you turn right.

② You could start the walk from here. Walk through the car park to reach a gate leading on to a broad track. This track leads up past the premises of the Banbury Sailing Club, after which the track becomes narrower and dives into a tunnel of trees. Byfield Pool Nature Reserve is on the left and you may like to follow the footpath alongside it for a short way. Continuing around the reservoir, you cross a footbridge and, shortly afterwards, bear right to come down to the water's edge. Following the obvious path under the trees, you reach the dam and cross over to its far side.

③ If you are circuiting the reservoir, turn right through the gate here, and continue on the path along the shores – this is a British Waterways permissive path. At its end, cross the north dam and continue on

---

PLACES OF INTEREST NEARBY

Heading east through Byfield and Woodford Halse will bring you to **Canons Ashby**, where the Elizabethan manor house is now under the care of the National Trust. Wall paintings, furniture and plasterwork are of interest inside, while outside there are formal gardens and a medieval priory church. Open from April to October. Telephone: 01327 860044.

Boddington Reservoir

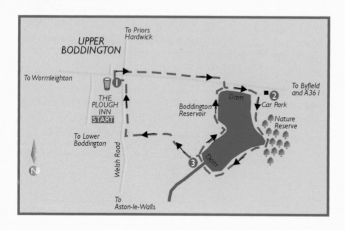

the field diagonally uphill to the right in the direction of a tall ash tree on the skyline. Reaching that tree, turn left and follow the path along the hedge to the road, where you turn right. You are now on Welsh Road, the route used by the drovers of the Middle Ages, bringing their cattle from Wales to the richer markets of London. Conjure up the images as you walk along it, and at the road junction, simply turn left for a few yards to reach the Plough.

the path behind the trees to the main car park.

To return to the Plough, from the end of the south dam, continue through the wooden kissing gate ahead. Then cross

Hellidon
The Red Lion

| MAP: OS LANDRANGER 151 OR EXPLORER 206 (GR 519581) | **WALK 19** | DISTANCE: $3\frac{1}{4}$ MILES |

DIRECTIONS TO START: FROM THE A361 DAVENTRY-BANBURY ROAD, TURN WEST AT CHARWELTON. TURN RIGHT (AFTER AROUND 2 MILES) WHERE SIGNED TO HELLIDON. THE RED LION IS AT THE ENTRANCE TO THE VILLAGE. **PARKING:** AT THE RED LION FOR PATRONS OR ON QUIET ROADSIDES NEARBY.

The rolling hills on the western borders of the county are known as the Northamptonshire Heights. Just to the east of Hellidon is Arbury Hill, at 738 ft the highest point in the county. Hellidon itself nestles at the foot of Windmill Hill and is a village of many attractive old properties. One of them, Leam House, sees the source of the River Leam in its cellar.

From Hellidon, the walk takes you to the fascinating hamlet of Lower Catesby, its dwellings grouped around a field where once a priory stood. The tiny church is built on the site of the priory chapel and has dark carved Jacobean pews and some of the finest medieval stained glass in the county. Beyond Lower Catesby, an avenue of limes leads up to Catesby House, a Victorian edifice incorporating building material from the old priory. From the hill behind, you can enjoy a fine view of the house and hamlet before returning to Hellidon.

The Red Lion

An old stone pub standing at the entrance to the village of Hellidon, the Red Lion presents an attractive sight on a summer's day with its garden of brightly coloured brollies. It is a view that has cheered the heart of many a walker on the Jurassic Way, which descends from the heights of Windmill Hill opposite. Inside there are lounges on different levels, beams, low ceilings and inglenook fireplaces. It is a justly popular place for a cosy Sunday lunch or evening dinner. But when the sun shines, eating outside is the order of the day and there is a good snack menu from Danish open sandwiches and baguettes to the real speciality of the house – farmhouse sausages! A variety of these are on offer (Cumberland, regency, royal smoked, beef and garlic) and many whole families come to enjoy the treat!

The Red Lion is a free house and serves a selection of ales including Ruddles and Courage Directors. Food is available here every day of the week from 12 noon to 2 pm and from 7 pm to 10 pm. Children are most welcome and well-behaved dogs are usually allowed floor space in the bar (although not too many at a time!). Telephone: 01327 261200.

The Walk

① From the Red Lion, turn right and follow Stockwell Lane through the village, passing many interesting properties and the old village well. At the junction, turn right and continue on the gated road to Lower Catesby. There are pleasant wide

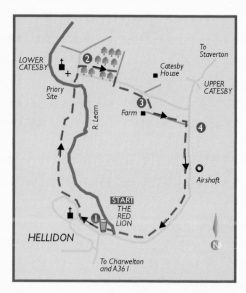

views as you go. After walking for about 15 minutes you reach some houses on the left hand side. The first has a beautiful garden with a large pond – this was once a fishpond of the priory.

② After passing the impressive converted coach house, you will see a track going off to the left. This leads to a fine house and, in the field opposite, the little church surrounded by a ha-ha (ditch) to keep out the grazing sheep. This field was once the site of the priory. Returning to the track junction, a footpath in the opposite direction leads through a field where an avenue of lime trees frames the distant Catesby House. Walk across the field between the limes and at the far side, turn right on the track to reach the road. Turn left, passing the newly-landscaped grounds of Catesby House.

③ Opposite the house, take a track on the right, heading uphill through the field. There are good views as you climb. At the top, keep straight ahead over a stile

Hellidon's old village well

onto a path alongside a field. A further stile brings you to a hollowed out field where cattle usually graze. Walk diagonally across the field, aiming for the

> ### PLACES OF INTEREST NEARBY
> Just down the road towards Byfield, a telecommunications tower sits on its hilltop. This is not quite the highest point in the county – Arbury Hill is just 6 ft higher – but it does have a splendid view across the Warwickshire plain to the west – and on a fine day you can see the Malvern Hills!

far right hand corner. Here steps take you up to a farm drive, where you turn left to reach a road.

④ Turn right on the road and follow it to Hellidon – a distance of about a mile. On the way you pass an airshaft from Catesby Tunnel. It is said that when the Great Central Railway was built in the 19th century, the then owner of Catesby House would not allow it to cross his parkland – so it had to go underneath! As you come into Hellidon, Leam House with the source of the Leam is on your right.

Badby
The Maltsters Country Inn

<table>
<tr><td>MAP: OS LANDRANGER 152 OR EXPLORER 206 (GR 559592)</td><td>WALK 20</td><td>DISTANCE: 2 MILES</td></tr>
</table>

DIRECTIONS TO START: BADBY LIES ABOIUT 2 MILES SOUTH OF DAVENTRY. FROM THE A361, TWO ROADS LEAD INTO THE VILLAGE – TAKE THE MOST NORTHERLY AND YOU WILL ALMOST IMMEDIATELY SEE THE MALTSTERS ON YOUR RIGHT. **PARKING:** AT THE MALTSTERS FOR PATRONS OR ON A QUIET ROADSIDE IN THE VILLAGE.

In a beautiful setting in the rolling hills of the Northamptonshire Heights, Badby is often cited as Northamptonshire's prettiest village (although there are other contestants!). The county's only Youth Hostel is situated here, below the 14th century stone church and before a green shaded by an old horse-chestnut. More fine chestnuts line the grassy banks in the lower part of the village where you will find the Maltsters Country Inn.

Just outside the village is Badby Wood, renowned for a magnificent bluebell display in springtime. But the burning colours of autumn beeches are just as exciting here – or you may prefer a bright winter morning with a white rime of frost on the trees. This short walk takes you right through the wood where there are many more paths to explore if you have the time.

The Maltsters Country Inn

This large inn is set high on a grassy slope, overlooking one of Badby's greens with its glorious horse-chestnut trees – you can take a table in one of the bay windows to get the best view. Inside, the bar and eating area are all one long room, with just a little subdivision. Low beams, carpets and simple décor are complemented by large stone fireplaces at each end – in winter one or two fires are lit according to the conditions outside, giving a welcoming feel.

The menu here is extensive at both lunchtime and evening, and changes by the day according to the whim of the chef. The current selection appears on chalkboards – on which there is no room for sandwiches, jackets etc, but they are all on offer. Hence to quote from this could be misleading, but you will always find vegetarian dishes, steaks, home-made soup and excellent savoury pies and puddings. In a friendly atmosphere, the food is attractively and very promptly served. The Maltsters is a free house with a similarly comprehensive range of ales to accompany the meal. Children (but not dogs) are welcome inside the inn, and suitably-sized portions are served. A pleasant garden caters for all in summer. Food is available every lunchtime and evening for most of the year, but not on Monday and Tuesday lunchtimes out of season. Telephone: 01327 702905.

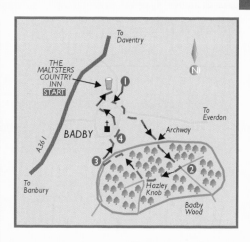

The Walk

① Leaving the Maltsters, turn right towards the village and then take the first road on the left (not the one opposite the pub). This is Chapel Lane (but you can't see its name) and soon you pass the old chapel, after which the road begins to climb. At the top of the hill a group of very old broken chestnuts stands on the right and behind them a broad track leads into the wood. Although there is an old Private Property notice, Fawsley Estate kindly allows the public free access to these woods. The track enters the woodland through an old archway. Ignore other tracks leading off and continue on this, the main track, to the top of the hill.

② At the track crossroads here, turn to the right. Again disregard other tracks – the track you are on descends and then climbs to a little knoll topped by an oak and some pines and beeches – Hazley Knob. To continue, bear just very slightly to the right across this hillock and look for the most substantial track descending on the far side. There are many possible ways of reaching the west side of the wood from here, but it is simplest to stick to this track, which reduces a little in width as you go. At length you arrive at a gully where pipes carry any water. Cross over,

The entrance to Badby Wood

and climb again to see the edge of the wood in front of you. Now turn left and, always keeping the edge of the wood in sight, climb for 5 minutes or so to arrive at a corner of woodland, where a stile in the fence and white disc on a pole proclaim that you have reached the Knightley Way.

③ Cross the stile to leave the wood. Follow the waymarkers across the field to a plank bridge to the left of a gate. Bear left around the edge of the next field to join a narrow sunken track taking you downhill and up again into Badby.

④ With the church in front of you, turn right and then left into Vicarage Hill. Descend to join the road at the bottom, and turn right to return to the Maltsters.

PLACES OF INTEREST NEARBY

Don't leave the area without a glance at some of the other pretty villages nearby – **Newnham**, **Everdon** and **Preston Capes** are all delightful and you could even stray as far south as **Eydon**, where the stone is dark red, and visit the nearby house at **Canons Ashby**, now owned by the National Trust (see Walk 18).

Braunston
The Admiral Nelson

MAP: OS LANDRANGER 152 OR EXPLORER 222 (GR 549659)

WALK 21

DISTANCE: $2^1/_2$ MILES

DIRECTIONS TO START: FROM DAVENTRY, TAKE THE A45 NORTH-WEST FOR 2 MILES. IMMEDIATELY AFTER THE CANAL BRIDGE, TURN RIGHT AND KEEP AHEAD THROUGH THE VILLAGE OF BRAUNSTON. ABOUT 300 YARDS AFTER THE FORK AT THE VILLAGE HALL, TURN RIGHT WHERE SIGNPOSTED TO LITTLE BRAUNSTON. THE NARROW ROAD GOES DOWN TO THE CANAL AND THE ADMIRAL NELSON. ALTERNATIVELY, APPROACH FROM THE A361 NORTH OF DAVENTRY, TURNING OFF WESTWARDS. **PARKING:** CARS CAN BE PARKED BESIDE THE CANAL NEAR THE ADMIRAL NELSON

Braunston is at the heart of Britain's inland waterways system, situated on its main artery, the Grand Union Canal, and connected to canals heading north, south, east and west. In the heyday of canal carrying, several companies had a base here and Braunston was considered 'home' for many of the itinerant canal families. All that is long gone, and the pleasure boats have taken over. Delightfully, many keep to the traditional design, with paintings of roses and castles, lots of gleaming brasswork and cabins full of china and lace.

Whatever the season there are always plenty of boats to be seen at Braunston. This walk also takes you past three locks, the marina, the old stop house where tolls were paid and the junction with the North Oxford Canal, with its classic Horsley Iron Works bridges. And after a pleasant return through the village and its Pocket Park, you finish up alongside the Grand Union again.

The Admiral Nelson

Pubs have always been an integral part of life on the boats and Braunston has at least three more of them, all of which you will pass on this route. But this is a canal walk and the Admiral Nelson is a canalside pub – here, either inside or out, you can enjoy a fine view of canal and lock along with your meal. Dating from 1730, the Admiral Nelson is old, but not olde worlde, a simple place of whitewashed walls and black beams. One side has now been made into a restaurant with curious brick arches known as the Cloisters. But it's the bar side that you want for a view of the water – or otherwise opt for one of the many outside tables, very popular with the boaters on a warm summer's evening.

The menu here is fairly standard, but garnished with a variety of home-made sauces – try, for example, chicken in pepper sauce or in Stilton and leek sauce. For lighter meals, ploughman's lunches and a variety of sandwiches are on offer. All the food is attractively presented and is pleasantly and promptly served. To go with the meal there is a very reasonable wine list and a range of ales including John Smith's cask bitter.

The Admiral Nelson serves food every lunchtime (12 noon to 2 pm) and on Monday to Saturday evenings (7 pm to 9 pm). Children are welcome but must confine themselves to the restaurant area, while dogs should definitely take their meals outside. Telephone: 01788 890075.

PLACES OF INTEREST NEARBY

For a complete change of scene, take a short drive north-east to **Ashby St Ledgers**, where the manor house (now private) was once owned by the Catesby family. It was in its half-timbered gatehouse that Robert Catesby and his associates hatched the Gunpowder Plot. Next door is a tiny church with fine medieval wall paintings and a three-tiered pulpit.

The Walk

① Leaving the Admiral Nelson beside the lock, cross over the bridge and turn right along the towpath. After passing two more locks, each followed by a bridge, you are opposite the old wharf where cargo was once loaded. Further on, steps and a bridge take you over the entrance to part of the marina. Finally you reach the main marina entrance, spanned by a splendid black and white bridge.

② Continue along the towpath passing the stop house on the left. It now houses exhibitions of art work and other canal related material. Along this stretch, traditionally painted boats will sell you anything from a dinner to a pair of earrings! Eventually you pass under the A45 and reach the canal junction. To the left, the Grand Union continues on its way to Birmingham – or, a few miles further along, you can choose to turn left to Oxford. But for this walk, just cross the bridges and continue ahead, now beside the North Oxford Canal, following the signpost to Coventry! Again pass under a road bridge and continue to the next bridge.

③ Cross the fence on the left and then cross the bridge itself. Now keep to the path along the edge of these lovely 'ridge

Braunston marina

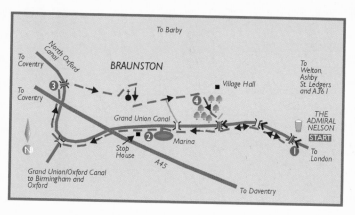

windmill, now a desirable residence. Reaching the main street, turn left and follow it through the village as far as the village hall on the corner.

④ On the opposite side of the road, cross the green and go down a narrow path between the houses. This passes through an area of woodland that is Braunston's Pocket Park. Keeping left through this, you enter a field with fine lime trees overlooking the canal. Walk down the field, cross the canal bridge and turn left along the towpath to retrace your steps to the Admiral Nelson.

and furrow' fields to reach the road at the top. The church is opposite. It has long been associated with the boating families – many are buried in the churchyard and their descendants still marry here. Turn left on the road and after about 150 yards, take a path on the right along the edge of the churchyard. To your left is an old

Bugbrooke
The Wharf Inn

MAP: OS LANDRANGER 152 OR EXPLORER 223 (GR 671569)	**WALK 22**	**DISTANCE:** 2$\frac{1}{2}$ MILES; SHORT CIRCUIT 1 MILE

DIRECTIONS TO START: TURN SOUTH OFF THE A45 AT THE ROUNDABOUT 3 MILES WEST OF NORTHAMPTON AND PASS THROUGH KISLINGBURY TO REACH BUGBROOKE. TURN RIGHT IN THE VILLAGE (SIGNPOSTED TO LITCHBOROUGH) AND CONTINUE AHEAD TO THE CANAL BRIDGE. THE WHARF INN IS ON THE FAR SIDE. **PARKING:** AT THE WHARF INN FOR PATRONS. ALTERNATIVELY, PARK IN THE VILLAGE AND START THE WALK AT POINT 3 BESIDE THE CHURCH.

Bugbrooke is a village well accustomed to travellers – the old Roman Watling Street passed close by as did an old drovers' road from Wales to London. The Grand Junction Canal arrived in 1796. But the heyday of the canals was short, their trade usurped by the railways. The London-Birmingham line was built in 1832, and passes south of Bugbrooke. Later the M1 was routed to the north.

It is the canal that is the main feature of this walk. The carrying trade has long-gone, but the Grand Union – which evolved from the Grand Junction – is still well used by leisure boaters. The circuit is completed with a stroll through Bugbrooke itself, passing the 14th century church and crossing the pretty Hoarstones Brook.

The Wharf Inn

At first glance, the Wharf Inn could be mistaken for an extension to the local primary school – neat rows of books lining the window sills enhance the effect! But don't be put off, it's well worth exploring further!

The inn stands beside the Grand Union Canal and started its life as the warehouses of the former wharf. Now there is no longer commercial traffic on the canal, the pleasure boaters arrive instead. Moorings are provided for them alongside the large garden, and if it's fine enough to sit outside, you can watch the manoeuvrings of passing craft as you dine. The pub itself has undergone a few changes since the old days. That low brick rather austere extension may not look much, but step inside! A full-sized red telephone kiosk greets you, and beyond it, a wonderfully atmospheric bar – low beams and generous woodwork, hanging mugs and work tools, and a cosy corner with a wood burning stove, piano, sofa and armchairs. Further on is a restaurant decked out as a library – hence the odd academic appearance from outside!

The food here is good, and as you might expect, interesting. Menus are displayed on the blackboard and food is served from 12 noon to 2 pm and 6 pm to 9.30 pm every day. There is also an à la carte menu in the evenings. Draught beers on offer include the local Frog Island, Morland Old Speckled Hen and Courage Best Bitter. Children are welcome inside – but dogs should remain in the garden. Telephone: 01604 832585.

The Walk

① Leaving the Wharf Inn, cross over the bridge and turn left to descend to the towpath (canal on the left). Enjoy the waterside walk as far as the next bridge – the lovely house on the left here was once a boaters' pub. Just under the bridge, take the steps uphill to join the road and turn left to meet the main road – ahead you can see Northampton Lighthouse (the local name for the Express Lifts tower, now disused) and to its left, the huge bulk of Heygates Flour Mill.

② The field on the opposite side offers two footpaths. Take the one bearing right, leading you across the end of a second field and then into a third field. Here again bear right to a stile between houses. A grassy track now takes you down to the main road again. Cross over and take a few paces to the right to arrive at the church – and a choice.

③ *For the short circuit – involving a brief scramble*, take the path through the

The 14th century church at Bugbrooke

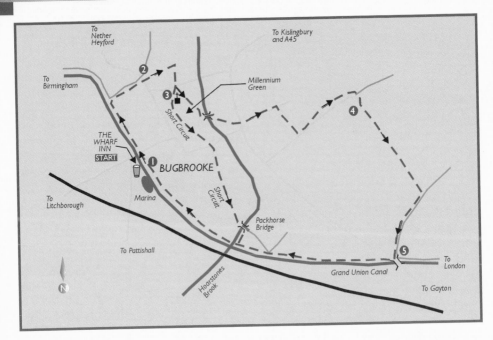

churchyard and around the back of the church. Continue ahead and leave the churchyard passing the Millennium wildlife garden on the left. Continue down West End and follow the field path ahead to cross Hoarstones Brook – the pillars are the remains of a 16th century packhorse bridge. Turn right alongside the brook and take a rough path climbing above the tunnel to reach the canal bank and turn right.

For the main walk, take the tarmacked path to the left of the church. Cross the brook and keep ahead to meet the main road at a junction. Cross to a tarmacked footpath opposite and continue through a close to meet a road. Turn right, and at the T-junction at the bottom of the hill, left. Continue around the bend to the end of the road.

④ Now continue ahead on the field path with the hedge first on your right, then on your left. Cross a short field to meet a broad track. Turn right on the track, which brings you to a road beside a canal bridge. Do not cross the bridge, but take a path on the left to descend to the towpath.

⑤ Turn right and follow the curving canal under two more bridges to arrive at Bugbrooke Wharf.

PLACES OF INTEREST NEARBY

Hunsbury Hill Country Park is 4 miles away, on the edge of Northampton and reached via the A45 going eastwards. The site of an Iron Age hill fort, it was quarried for ironstone in the 19th century. Old locomotives have now been restored and you can take a ride along the former tracks and investigate the open-air museum. Telephone: 01604 702444.

Great Brington
The Fox and Hounds

MAP: OS LANDRANGER 152 OR EXPLORER 223 (GR 666649)	**WALK 23**	DISTANCE: 4 MILES; SHORT CIRCUIT 1½ MILES

DIRECTIONS TO START: TURN OFF THE A428 NORTHAMPTON-RUGBY ROAD 2 MILES NORTH-WEST OF HARLESTONE, SIGNPOSTED TO ALTHORP. AT THE CHURCH IN GREAT BRINGTON, BEAR LEFT DOWN THE VILLAGE STREET. THE FOX AND HOUNDS IS ON THE RIGHT. **PARKING:** AT THE FOX AND HOUNDS FOR PATRONS. OTHERWISE, PARK WITH CARE IN THE VILLAGE STREET.

The lovely brown stone dwellings of Great Brington once housed the workers on the nearby Althorp estate, the home of the Spencer family. The little sleepy village gained the attention of the world when Lady Diana died tragically in a car crash in the summer of 1997. She was to have been buried in the Spencer Chapel of the village church, but it was thought that the continued influx of visitors would be too much for Great Brington. Instead she lies on an island in the lake on the family estate, and it is possible to view the site – and other Diana memorabilia – for just two months each year. To enjoy the peace of this route, it might be as well to avoid that time!

The walk is divided into two parts. The first is a stroll along a lovely grassy path to the gates of Althorp House, returning along a quiet road with views of the house and parkland. For the more energetic, a further ramble from Great Brington across the rolling countryside takes you to Little Brington – and you can compare the two.

The Fox and Hounds

The lovely ironstone Fox and Hounds has been serving ales since the 16th century, and was once a coaching inn – the way to the car park lies through the old stone archway and across the one-time stable yard. In summer time, that yard is decked with hanging vines and garnished with pots of geraniums and fuchsias – a delightful place to enjoy an alfresco meal, as is the little apple orchard at the back. But if it's a day for dining inside you won't be disappointed – old beams and brassware, hunting horns, books, pictures, farm implements, barrels, cartwheels and a roaring log fire in winter are just some of the attractions.

The food is first-class, as you might expect, and overall tends to the top of the normal range with, for example, 'half lobster with prawns in garlic sauce'. For lesser fare, delicious open sandwiches, baguettes and ploughman's lunches are on offer, all very well presented. There is an excellent accompanying range of ales, including Morland Old Speckled Hen, Fuller's London Pride and Everards Tiger, and there are guest beers. Children are welcomed here and have their own menu – and dogs may enjoy with their owners the atmosphere of the bar. Telephone: 01604 770651.

The Walk

① Leaving the Fox and Hounds, walk downhill and where the road swings right, continue ahead on Hamilton Lane. In just a few yards, take a track on the left, signposted to Harlestone. This track soon becomes grassy and runs between fields with wide views. Away on the right you can see the spire of Little Brington, a church now without a nave. Eventually the track runs through woodland and emerges on a tarmacked road.

② Ahead is the wall of Althorp Park and if you walk a hundred yards or so to the right you can see the fine stone gates. To continue with the walk, turn and continue uphill with the estate wall on your right. The house can be clearly seen across the parkland – at one point the wall seems to be cut out just to give you a view! Follow this quiet road all the way up to the church – on the way you pass an avenue of oak trees, evidently once lining the family's route from the house. At the road junction, turn left around the lovely ironstone church – the Spencer Chapel projects from the building on this side.

③ The parting of the ways. To return to the Fox and Hounds, simply keep ahead and enjoy the lovely houses of the village street. To continue with the walk (a further $2^1/_2$ miles), turn right, signposted to Whilton. There are interesting views of two curiously tree-topped hills, Gawburrow and Thornburrow. Take the

PLACES OF INTEREST NEARBY

Althorp House is open in July and August, when you can have access to 16 rooms in the house and to the exhibition based on Princess Diana's life. The house is open from 9 am to noon and 1pm to 5 pm each day. Telephone: 01604 770107. Five miles to the north, the landscaped gardens of **Coton Manor** are open on summer afternoons (except Monday and Tuesday). Telephone: 01604 740219.

second footpath on the left, which climbs round the side of Gawburrow Hill, dips down and climbs again through fields to reach a broad, earthy track.

④ Cross this track and cross the next field along the line of the telegraph poles. Gates (and white discs on poles) lead you along the sides of the next two fields and across the third. In the fourth field, you are joined by the Macmillan Way and the route ahead to Little Brington is quite obvious. Emerging on the village street, turn left. At the road junction, turn left and walk along the pavement all the way back to Great Brington.

The entrance to Althorp House

Chapel Brampton
The Spencer Arms

MAP: OS LANDRANGER 152 OR EXPLORER 223 (GR 732662)

WALK 24

DISTANCE: 3½ MILES

DIRECTIONS TO START: CHAPEL BRAMPTON IS JUST NORTH OF NORTHAMPTON ON THE A5199 LEICESTER ROAD. APPROACHING FROM THE SOUTH, THE SPENCER ARMS IS ON THE RIGHT, JUST BEFORE THE CROSSROADS. **PARKING:** AT THE SPENCER ARMS FOR PATRONS OR ON QUIET ROADSIDES IN THE VILLAGE.

Chapel Brampton rose to fame at the end of the 18th century when it became a major staging post on the Irish mail run. You pass the Old Posting House as you set out on this walk. The village, and its twin, Church Brampton, were once 'estate villages' belonging to the Spencers at nearby Althorp.

This easy ramble passes through both the Bramptons, and then climbs a low hill with fine views all around. In the valley ahead is the River Brampton, on its way to join the Nene in Northampton. The route takes you down beside the river on the Brampton Valley Way, an old railway track, now hard-surfaced for walkers and cyclists. And you end by passing the restored Pitsford and Brampton Station with its collection of rolling stock from bygone days.

The Spencer Arms

This was once the Stag's Head, a real old village alehouse. Not so today! Although it is now a fairly large establishment belonging to the Chef and Brewer group, inside there is still plenty of atmosphere with low-beamed ceilings, two open fires (genuine!) in winter, and a collection of Spencer memorabilia decking the walls. It is a popular place and in line with this, the menu is certainly extensive. Walkers' snacks are well catered for in the form of jacket potatoes, sandwiches (three inches thick!), hot baguettes and soup. But if you feel like upgrading a bit, you could opt for green-lipped mussels, quails eggs or perhaps roast pheasant.

Food is available all day, every day (at least, from 11 am to 10 pm on weekdays and from 12 noon to 9 pm on Sundays) and a selection of real ales is on offer, including a guest ale. Children are welcomed inside and out, but dogs will have to settle for the garden. Telephone: 01604 842237.

The Walk

① From the Spencer Arms, walk along the road into the village and go straight over at the crossroads. After passing Cedar Hythe, the 'Spencer Ten' houses are on your right and the Old Posting House is opposite. Cross the road and walk up along its side. The one-time mews behind has now been converted to housing. Where the road swings left, cross it and continue on the track ahead beside gardens and then across a field. At the far hedge, turn left for a few yards and then right, now following a path beside

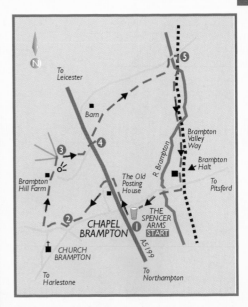

the hedge which comes out through a gate to the main road. Continue to the crossroads.

② Here turn right in the direction of Holdenby. Take great care as there is no footpath around a blind corner. Pass the entrance to stables and then take a footpath into the field on the right. The path climbs to the farm at the top of the hill, from where there are good views. At the cross-tracks in front of its gates, go straight ahead and in about 200 yards, reach a major track junction.

③ Now turn right and walk along with the hedge on your left (although the horses have obviously chosen the opposite side). Continue across the field to the farm access road. Turn left on this to reach the main road.

④ Cross the road and turn left. After about 50 yards take the cross-field footpath to the right. If its direction is

The restored Pitsford and Brampton railway station

PLACES OF INTEREST NEARBY

Two miles away, on the road to East Haddon, is **Holdenby House** – built by Sir Christopher Hatton, a favourite of Elizabeth I, as a suitable place to entertain Her Majesty. Charles I was later imprisoned here. In a place 'alive with history', superb gardens, a falconry centre, armoury and farmstead enhance the visit. Telephone: 01604 770074. The **Northampton and Lamport Railway** runs trains from Pitsford and Brampton Station on Sunday afternoons – the route follows the Brampton Valley Way and the ride takes about 20 minutes. Telephone: 01604 820327.

unclear, cross the first field to its opposite corner, cross the footbridge over the ditch, and maintain your direction across the second field. (You can avoid field-walking altogether, if you wish – see map.) This brings you to a narrow road, where you turn right to cross the river and reach the Brampton Valley Way.

⑤ Turn right on the Brampton Valley Way and continue to the Pitsford and Brampton Station, the base of the Northampton and Lamport Railway – about ¹/₂ mile. It's a scene of activity in summer and the station itself has a snack bar and a restaurant, the Brampton Halt. Go through the station to the road, where a right turn will soon take you back to Chapel Brampton.

West Haddon
The Pytchley Inn

MAP: OS LANDRANGER 140 OR EXPLORER 223 (GR 631718)

WALK 25

DISTANCE: 4 MILES

DIRECTIONS TO START: WEST HADDON LIES ON THE A428 NORTHAMPTON-RUGBY ROAD, 4 MILES EAST OF ITS JUNCTION WITH THE M1. THE PYTCHLEY INN IS ON THAT ROAD, AT ITS JUNCTION WITH THE ROAD TO GUILSBOROUGH. **PARKING:** AT THE PYTCHLEY INN FOR PATRONS, OTHERWISE ROADSIDE IN THE VILLAGE.

In the north-west of the county, West Haddon is set amid rolling agricultural farmland. The land here is high by Northamptonshire standards, and rising to its peak at Honey Hill (702 ft), 3 miles north of West Haddon.

The walk first takes you across the fields to the very pretty but remote hamlet of Winwick with a little stream beside its street. You can take time to look at the 13th century church and the Elizabethan Manor House, where once lived Sir Thomas Malory, the author of *Morte d'Arthur*. The village also boasts Winwick Hall, dating from 1850, a Victorian postbox, and a millennium seat beside a pond where you might like to rest your legs before climbing the hill to the east as you return to West Haddon.

The Pytchley Inn

This Georgian building of impressive proportions has been an inn offering accommodation for the past 60 years or so. The imposingly pillared doorway seems a far cry from the usual village pub – but once through it, you enter a bar that is as homely and welcoming as any. Divided rooms, low beams, walls decorated with pictures and plate and (on cold days) a burning gas fire create a comfortable atmosphere in which to enjoy a meal. And if you prefer to dine where there is no smoking, the Ascot Room is a complete contrast, retaining its Georgian elegance with high ceilings, pillars, drapes and cut-glass lightshades.

The Pytchley Inn is justly popular, offering excellent value with a wide choice of fare. All the usual jackets and ploughman's lunches, steaks, chicken and fish dishes appear on the regular menu but each day also has its selection of 'Chef's Specials' chalked on the boards – the likes of lamb shank steak and fillet of salmon. The chef has his dessert specials too – 'Irish and Cream, a chocolate mousse with vanilla and Irish ice-cream sprinkled with nuts and chocolate' seemed to be going down well when we called! Ales on offer include John Smith's and Theakston XB, but there is also a most affordable wine list. Children are welcomed at the Pytchley Inn – and have their own menu – but dogs should not venture further than the beer garden. Food is served every day from 12 noon to 2 pm and 6 pm to 10 pm (9.30 pm on Sundays). Telephone: 01788 510426.

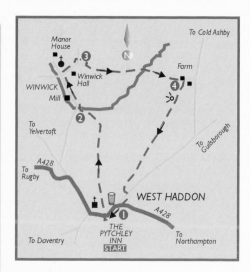

The Walk

① Leaving the Pytchley Inn, turn right down the street. Just before the Crown Inn, turn right up Crown Lane – you are now on the Jurassic Way and can follow its shell signs all the way through to Winwick. At the end of the path a kissing gate leads you into a field. Keep ahead to the top (ignore the gate on your left) and then continue with the hedge on your left. Cross the next large field directly, and in the next field, bear left through a hedge to briefly join a track. Now cross the field to go through a waymarked white gate on the left.

② Keep ahead on the lane into Winwick, passing Winwick Mill. At the junction beside the bridge, the church and Manor House are at the end of the road ahead. When you return, turn up the road beside the white thatched cottage and walk uphill, passing the Victorian postbox and Winwick Hall.

③ At the pond and seat, bear right, and at the end of the lane go through a gate on

Winwick, visited on the walk

the left. Turn right immediately on an obvious field track (leaving the Jurassic Way to go ahead). The grassy track goes uphill, down across the brook, and uphill again to reach White House Farm at the top. Here you go through a gate and immediately turn right. There are views all round and you can see the radio masts at Rugby.

④ Follow the waymarks straight across two fields, and then bear slightly right downhill across the next two. Now climb again, aiming just right of the corrugated iron barn. Go through a gate beside it and turn right on a plank bridge across a stream. In the next big field, keep the hedge on your right all the way (ignore the path going left before the brick building). Head for a gap in the wire fencing before the houses and then turn left to reach the road. Turn right along the road to return to West Haddon and the Pytchley Inn at the road junction.

PLACES OF INTEREST NEARBY

For more views, you might like to visit **Honey Hill**. The Jurassic Way is heading there after Winwick – but you could reach it more comfortably by driving to Cold Ashby and turning left on the road to Stanford-on-Avon. You can park the car beside the road and follow the track across the hill with splendid views to the north.

Lamport
The Lamport Swan

MAP: OS LANDRANGER 141 OR EXPLORER 223 (GR 755745)

WALK 26

DISTANCE: $3\frac{1}{2}$ MILES

DIRECTIONS TO START: THE LAMPORT SWAN IS ON THE A508 NORTHAMPTON-MARKET HARBOROUGH ROAD, 3 MILES SOUTH OF ITS JUNCTION WITH THE A14. **PARKING:** AT THE LAMPORT SWAN FOR PATRONS OR ON QUIET ROADSIDES IN THE VILLAGE.

The little stone village of Lamport is dominated by its Hall, an ornate edifice originally dating from the 16th century, but 'modernised' in Georgian times. For over 400 years, it belonged to the Isham family, on whose coat of arms appears a swan – hence the twin swans on the gateposts, and the name of the interesting old village pub.

Lamport is set in attractively rolling countryside and you have pleasant views from the outset of this walk. The route includes a section of the Brampton Valley Way, the track bed of the old Northampton to Market Harborough railway, which is now managed as a linear park. From here you climb the hill to the old village of Hanging Houghton. For those who want a quick return along the road, Lamport is but a few minutes away – but the more interesting route is through the green parkland of Lamport Hall.

The Lamport Swan

This impressively-sized inn seems far too large for the tiny village of Lamport. The explanation is that back in the 18th century, this was a very busy establishment – a staging post on the London to York road. Three hundred years on, it still sits on its hill overlooking the Brampton valley, a view you can enjoy from the outside tables on a sunny summer's day. On less balmy days, there is a warm welcome inside where meals can be taken in both the bar and the restaurant – of which only the latter has a no smoking area. The atmosphere is very informal and children are welcome – although, sadly, not dogs.

The menu here is quite extensive, with some unusual starters, for example you could choose Bantry Bay mussels with white wine, garlic, shallots and cream, or mushrooms with pepper sauce and Stilton. But if it is just a snack you have in mind, baguettes, burgers, jackets and the like are on offer every day except Sunday, when there is a carvery instead. There is a good range of real ales including Pedigree, Directors and Theakston Best Bitter. An added bonus for walkers is that meals are served throughout the day at weekends; to be more precise, food is served from 12 noon to 2 pm on weekdays and from 12 noon to 9 pm on Saturdays and Sundays. Telephone: 01604 686555.

The Walk

① Leaving the Lamport Swan, walk downhill on the footpath beside the

---

> ### PLACES OF INTEREST NEARBY
> **Lamport Hall** contains an outstanding collection of furniture, books and paintings. It is set in pleasant parkland and gardens. Sir Charles Isham imported the first garden gnomes from Germany here – and gave them a home in his curious rock garden. The Hall is open in the afternoons from Easter to October. Telephone: 01604 686272.

A508, enjoying attractive views over the undulating countryside. In about 300 yards, take the footpath across the field on the left and continue descending beside the hedge to reach the Brampton Valley Way.

② Here turn left and follow this hard-surfaced track for $^2/_3$ mile to Hanging Houghton junction. The rural views are pleasant and there are strategically placed seats for you to enjoy them.

③ At this junction, turn left and climb the narrow road to Hanging Houghton. On your right is the gently rounded Clint

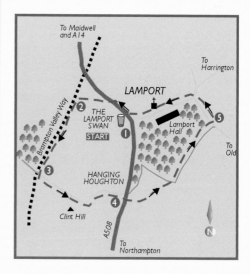

The delightful view from the pub's garden

Hill, while on the left a large farm looks out over the valley (Houghton is derived from the Saxon, meaning farm on a spur). Continue through the village – a blend of old and new – to reach the main road.

④ If you want a short return, follow the road to the left – there is a footpath all the way, and 10 minutes or so will bring you to the pub. To carry on with the ramble, cross over the road and take the bridleway almost directly opposite. This broad track follows the hedge on the left hand side of the field. Before you reach the cross-hedge, a footpath sign points through the hedge on your left and across a huge field to a gate on the far side. The horses have quite obviously gone straight on and turned left at the cross-hedge – take your choice. Whatever you do, you eventually arrive at that distant gate, which admits you to the parkland of Lamport Hall. Continue across the springy turf, keeping alongside the fence to reach the road beside the lodge.

⑤ Turn left on the road and walk alongside the stone wall to the road junction. Turn left here and continue through the village, passing the squat-towered old church with the Hall behind its wall on the opposite side of the road. Just a few yards further on, the Lamport Swan stands beside the road junction.

Marston Trussell
The Sun Inn

| MAP: OS LANDRANGER 141 OR EXPLORER 223 (GR 692859) | **WALK 27** | DISTANCE: $3\frac{1}{2}$ MILES |

DIRECTIONS TO START: TURN SOUTH OFF THE A4304, JUST TO THE WEST OF LUBENHAM, SIGNPOSTED TO MARSTON TRUSSELL. **PARKING:** AT THE SUN INN FOR PATRONS OR ON ROADSIDES IN THE VILLAGE.

The tiny village of Marston Trussell has nestled beside the infant River Welland for over a thousand years. It was originally Merston, and the 'Trussell' was added in the Middle Ages to commemorate the landowning family of the time. Marston's most notable son and benefactor was one Mark Brewster, a pirate who terrorised the Baltic before 'settling down' in this out-of-the-way spot. The Russians tracked him down even here, and he was executed for his crimes. His memorial stands in the church – where you can also see a 13th

century chest, and hunt for the fascinating Mason and Merchant marks left in the stonework by the builders of the same era.

The walk from here follows the banks of the Welland and crosses the attractive grounds of Thorpe Lubenham Hall. Climbing a hill, you have a fine view over the river valley and can seek out the intriguing Judith Stone before you return. The huge glacial boulder apparently marked the limits of the lands of Judith, Countess of Huntingdon, in the 12th century.

The Sun Inn

The Sun Inn is an old establishment – its history goes back to the 1645 Battle of Naseby, in which it was said to have been occupied by Parliamentarian forces. A skirmish occurred in the field opposite when Royalists retreating from that battle were trapped by the Roundheads here. Those who fell that day are buried in the churchyard across the road.

Coming back to present times, the Sun is also a small hotel. Nevertheless, it has a very warm welcome for walkers – which, in the best traditions of an old hostelry, it also extends to their canine companions (if well-behaved!). Children, too, are welcome, but unfortunately there is no garden, just a few pleasant outside tables at the front of the building. Food is varied and of high quality – 'snack' meals such as soups, salads and ciabatta sandwiches are on offer as well as very much more exotic fare in the restaurant. This is a free house and beverages include Ruddles Best, Foster's and Strongbow cider. Food is served from 12 noon to 9.30 pm every day. Telephone: 01858 465531.

The Walk

① With the Sun Inn on your left, walk up the road towards Market Harborough, passing the church on the right. After about 10 minutes' walking, the road crosses the Welland. About 50 yards after this, look for a kissing gate in the hedge on the right. This takes you into a riverside meadow, where you follow the bank of the river downstream to reach another brick bridge.

PLACES OF INTEREST NEARBY

If you are interested in the Civil War, head south from Marston Trussell through Sibbertoft to **Naseby**. About 1½ miles south of Sibbertoft a track leads uphill to a monument overlooking the battlefield. A further monument (wrongly sited!) is on the Clipston road. And although only open on bank holiday weekends, the tiny **Naseby Farm Museum** on the Cottesbrooke road is well worth a visit.

② Leave the field, cross the bridge and climb a stile on the left. This field is now the parkland of Thorpe Lubenham Hall and you cross it diagonally. Aim first for a small spinney of oaks in the middle of the field and then maintain your direction to the far corner.

③ Leaving the field, turn right on the road. After passing the grounds of Thorpe Lubenham Hall you reach open fields on either side. After about 30 yards, look for a path crossing the field on the right – you can find it by following the direction of the fingerpost across the grassland on the left. The path takes you to the top corner of the field, after which you follow beside the right hand hedge of two fields that have open access under the Countryside Commission. There are fine views back over the Welland valley to Market Harborough.

④ At the next cross-hedge do not go through the gateway. Your way lies to the right – but first follow the hedge to the left uphill to find the Judith Stone in a hollow in the field. Returning, keep straight ahead past the gateway and continue into the next field. The broad

The Judith Stone

grassy track along its edge is a bridleway and this continues along the edge of two more fields. At the track junction with an entrance to the estate on the right, turn left and follow the bridleway along the hedge to the road.

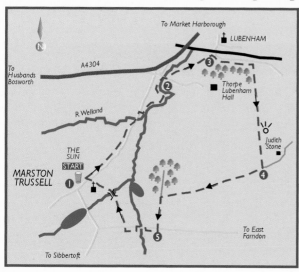

⑤ Turn right on the narrow road and, after about 500 yards, cross a field on the right diagonally, following the direction of a fingerpost. At its opposite corner, cross the stream into the church field. Now head towards a stile in the wall of the churchyard – notice the undulations marking the site of a small medieval castle on your right as you reach the wall. And as you pass the church, cast a glance at the porch (although it's worth going through if you have time). The arched wooden timbers are thought to have come from a Danish ship once stranded on the Welland.

Arthingworth
The Bull's Head

<table>
<tr><td>MAP: OS LANDRANGER 141 OR EXPLORER 223 (GR 755813)</td><td>WALK 28</td><td>DISTANCE: 3 MILES</td></tr>
</table>

DIRECTIONS TO START: TURN NORTH-EAST OFF THE A508 AT KELMARSH, ABOUT A MILE NORTH OF ITS JUNCTION WITH THE A14. THE BULL'S HEAD IS ON THE LEFT AS YOU COME INTO ARTHINGWORTH.
PARKING: AT THE BULL'S HEAD FOR PATRONS OR ON QUIET ROADSIDES IN THE VILLAGE.

From the top of its hillock, Arthingworth looks out across the gentle valley of the River Ise. This is an ancient village, but very few of its old dwellings remain – the Bull's Head is one of them.

From Arthingworth, a short stroll beside the infant river brings you to the attractive Brampton Valley Way, a linear park along the former track bed of the Northampton to Market Harborough railway. This is a particularly exciting stretch where the track enters a deep cutting, and then disappears into the Oxendon tunnel, over 400 yards long. Don't forget your torches! The return is over the hill above, the highest point for miles around. From here there are distant views in every direction, and you can look across to the neighbouring hill, from where the houses of Arthingworth beckon you home.

The Bull's Head

This is a large establishment for such a tiny village as Arthingworth. But it attracts clientele from far and wide with its welcoming and friendly atmosphere and wide-ranging menu. Sunday lunch is very popular!

The rather austere exterior is soon forgotten once inside – the large room is divided into a bar area where the walls are decorated with an abundance of farm implements and tools and various eating rooms where you can admire plates, brassware, mugs and the rest. The menu here always includes home-made soup, jackets and other 'snacks' – and there is a particularly good range for vegetarians (for example, cauliflower cheese pastie and cheese and vegetable bake). Main meals include mixed grill, gammon, steak and ale pie, and a few 'different' dishes such as Italian beef and potato skins.

The Bull's Head is a free house and offers a guest ale in addition to Everards Tiger, Beacon and others. There is an outside eating area for warm weather, but children are very welcome inside the pub – and even dogs have their own corner. Food is served every lunchtime (12 noon to 2.30 pm on weekdays, 12 noon to 4 pm on Saturday and Sunday) and evening (6.30 pm to 9 pm or thereabouts). Telephone: 01858 525637.

The Walk

① From the Bull's Head, walk uphill to the road junction and turn left up Oxenden Road into the village. Follow the road uphill and down until at its end,

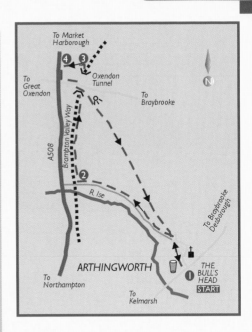

you reach open fields. Now continue on the hard-surfaced track, which soon brings you beside the River Ise and then goes on between fields to reach the Brampton Valley Way.

② Turn right on the Brampton Valley Way and keep ahead between the banks for about ¹/₂ mile to the tunnel entrance. You can see light at the far end (and there are a couple of air vents en route), but it is very dark in there and it will take you five or six minutes to walk through. At the far side, turn left (signposted 'Macmillan Way') before you reach the overhead brick bridge.

③ Walk back up the wooded banks towards the tunnel mouth. Before crossing the entrance, turn right (now on the Macmillan Way and the Jurassic Way), cross the stile into a field and continue diagonally across it. Cross the next small

Along the Brampton Valley Way

field similarly to reach a track leading to the main road.

④ At the main road, turn left and walk down to take the next road on the left, the road to Braybrooke. Pass the houses and, just in front of a brick garage on the right, take the footpath leading into the field. This climbs uphill to the right of the ventilation shaft. The fields at the top have open access under the Countryside Commission and there are some splendid views. You can see Arthingworth on the hill ahead, and the line of the footpath you want is approximately just to the right of it, passing through gaps in the field hedges on the way. Finally you cross a bridge over a brook beneath a large oak tree and walk diagonally across the last field to join the track on which you set out. Return through the village to the Bull's Head.

PLACES OF INTEREST NEARBY

If you drive along to Desborough (3 miles) and continue in the direction of Rushton, you can take a look at the very curious **Triangular Lodge**. Built by Sir Thomas Tresham in the late 16th century, it was designed on the theme of the Trinity (three sides, three floors, three windows on each), an imaginitive monument to his Catholic faith. And unique in Northamptonshire, **Coughton Galleries** in the Old Manor House at Arthingworth are truly for the art connoisseur.

Stoke Albany
The White Horse

| MAP: OS LANDRANGER 141 OR EXPLORER 224 (GR 807877) | **WALK 29** | DISTANCE: 2 MILES |

DIRECTIONS TO START: STOKE ALBANY IS 3 MILES WEST OF CORBY, JUST OFF THE A427. ALTERNATIVELY IT CAN BE REACHED FROM THE A6 BY TURNING NORTHWARDS WHERE SIGNED NORTH OF DESBOROUGH. THE WHITE HORSE IS AT THE CROSSROADS AT THE TOP OF THE VILLAGE. **PARKING:** PATRONS ARE WELCOME TO PARK AT THE WHITE HORSE, OTHERWISE FIND A QUIET ROADSIDE.

The great cities and towns of America are built on a grid of interlocking streets. Stoke Albany got there first! Way back in the 12th century, it was designed by lord of the manor William de Albini (hence Albany) with parallel lanes leading off the main street – and those lanes are much more imaginatively named than their numerical American counterparts. Green Lane, Middle Lane, Chapel Lane and Bottom Lane, each flanked by delightful thatched cottages, still succeed each other down the hill. At the bottom is an attractive 13th century church in Northamptonshire ironstone.

Just a few minutes walk from Stoke Albany brings you to the village of Wilbarston. Here the church is at the top of the hill, its spire reaching into the sky – but the stone is still that glorious deep orange colour. After a stroll down a lane of old cottages, a short field path over the hill returns you to the White Horse.

The White Horse

The friendly White Horse has served locals and travellers in Stoke Albany for more than a hundred years. Inside, its stone walls and low-beamed ceilings proclaim the building itself to be several times that age. The floor is on several levels – you can dine on the 'balcony' or retreat to the farthest end where in winter the huge brick fireplace sports a suitably-sized log fire. This little pub has room for only a few diners – nevertheless, the excellent cuisine ensures that the handful of tables are occupied even on the most inclement of nights. In summer, the dining accommodation is extended to the pleasant small garden with its water feature.

On the surface, the menu looks fairly standard – although ham and marmalade rolls are certainly novel! But much of this food is home-made, with the liberal use of cheeses such as Brie and Stilton – the turkey and Stilton pie is simply delicious! Side-salads are generous and most attractively served, vegetarians are well catered for and there is an appropriate children's menu. A selection of real ales and an affordable wine list complete the picture. The White Horse serves food every lunchtime and evening with a popular carvery on Sunday – but if it's just a snack you want on that day, you can enjoy the same hot meat in a crusty roll. Telephone: 01858 535268.

The Walk

① Leaving the White Horse, cross the road and walk down Ashley Road opposite.

PLACES OF INTEREST NEARBY

East Carlton Countryside Park is 2 miles east along the A427. Here a French-style chateau is surrounded by glorious parkland – curiously dotted with relics of the local iron-ore industry. The outbuildings house an exhibition of iron-ore mining, along with various craft shops and a café. Outside is a children's play area and the park has pleasant views across the Welland valley.

Take a look at those handsome thatched stone cottages in the lanes leading off on the left. On the right a very old manor house with stone mullioned windows looks out over the valley. At the bottom of the hill an attractive scene awaits you – beside the village green stands the church with its low tower and the old school, now the village hall. Turn right here and continue on the road.

② After about 300 yards, a fingerpost on the right directs you across the field. Now you cross the stream on a little bridge and climb to a gate in the wall of Wilbarston church at the top of the hill. Walk through the churchyard to the road, and turn right to reach the main road beside the Fox Inn. Cross the road directly and walk down Main Street, a street lined by old houses of rich-coloured ironstone. At the crossroads, turn right down Barlow's Lane with more cottages, and continue to the farm and house at its end.

③ Go through the gate into the field beside the house and cross the brook at the bottom of the hill. Now walk up the field, heading slightly to the right if the path is not clear. As you climb, a church spire comes into view – that of Brampton

Stoke Albany

Ash about a mile away. Head straight towards it and you will soon see again the village of Stoke Albany with the White Horse on its corner. Continue down to a stile that takes you to the road below. Turn left to return to the White Horse.

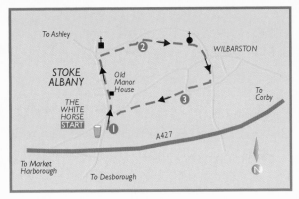

Wakerley
The Exeter Arms

MAP: OS LANDRANGER 141 OR EXPLORER 224 (GR 955995)	WALK 30	DISTANCE: 2$\frac{1}{2}$ MILES; CIRCUIT IN THE WOOD 1$\frac{1}{2}$ MILES

DIRECTIONS TO START: WAKERLEY IS 5 MILES SOUTH OF STAMFORD AND LIES JUST WEST OF THE A43. THE EXETER ARMS IS ON THE LEFT ON ENTERING THE VILLAGE. FROM THE PUB, DRIVE UP THE ROAD PAST THE CHURCH TO REACH THE CAR PARKS IN THE WOOD. **PARKING:** AT THE EXETER ARMS FOR PATRONS, OR AT THE WELL-SIGNED WOODLAND CAR PARKS (AT POINT 4 ON THE MAP).

Close by the village of Wakerley is Wakerley Great Wood, one of the largest remaining tracts of the ancient Rockingham Forest. This was a royal hunting forest and the deer are still plentiful today. Forest Enterprise has developed the wood for recreation and you will find clearings with picnic tables and even barbecues. There are also waymarked forest trails and a permanent orienteering course.

The route described here is just a short amble along well-trodden forest paths. You can choose to start from the car parks in the wood itself, but if you start at the pub, you will first cross a field beside the old church of St John the Baptist. The church is no longer used for worship – but take a look at the ornate heavy ironwork on the door! It is said that in the Middle Ages, gangs of bandits roamed the forest. From time to time the villagers needed to take refuge in the church – and that door could not be broken down!

The Exeter Arms

This is an establishment in the best tradition of British pubs. Simply furnished and homely, it offers a warm welcome to everyone, with home-made food and a good range of beers on tap. The name of the pub comes from the Cecil family who adopted the title Earls of Exeter. Some 300 years ago, their splendid manor house stood across the road, but after a series of misfortunes, they abandoned it in favour of Burghley House near Stamford. You can still see the remains – just a few humps and hollows in the field opposite.

Being now on the long-distance Jurassic Way, the Exeter Arms is no stranger to walking parties. Those who arrive here in the cold or wet enjoy the comforts of the wood-burning stove in the lounge, while the many outside tables come into their own in the height of summer. Children are made to feel at home both inside and out, and dogs are afforded the same courtesy but confined to the bar area.

The menu here is not extensive, but the fare is affordable and interestingly served. Meals are served at lunchtime and in the evening every day except Sunday. Sadly, this first-class pub is under threat of closure – but this has been the case for some time now, and with the added support of 'pub strollers' may hopefully never happen! But to be sure of your meal, it would be best to phone and check! Telephone: 01572 747817. (Should this pub close, just a mile away in Barrowden is a pub of the same name, also serving excellent food.)

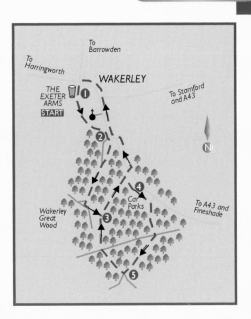

The Walk

① From the car park of the Exeter Arms, walk up some steps into the field behind. The footpath crosses the field behind the church and comes out on the road. Turn right and continue uphill to the corner.

② Leave the road here and walk through the little car park. Continue ahead on a narrow path leading into the wood. This climbs uphill and is joined by a track on the right (coming from the edge of the field). Keep ahead for 6 or 7 minutes until a stand of tall pines can be seen on the left. The path forks – bear left and a few yards farther on, in front of a gully, left again. In a minute or two you reach a fork of main tracks. Keep left again on a path that brings you to a cross-tracks.

③ Turn left here on a narrower path with trees crowding on either side. This eventually comes out at an old tarmacked area. Continue ahead and to

In Wakerley Great Wood

the right to reach the main car parks. (You could start from here rather than the pub.)

④ Keep ahead past the car parks to the main entrance. Turn right, and through the barrier, take a wide sandy track. It is bordered by a variety of trees including oak, ash, silver birch, field maple and pine. As the track bends to the right another track crosses. Keep on the main track here and continue to the next cross-tracks.

⑤ Turn right here and take a narrower track climbing uphill through deciduous woodland. At the top of the hill a track crosses, but you keep ahead. Soon you come to Point 3, a point you passed earlier if you started at the pub. Continue ahead to the tarmacked area.

If you are returning to the car park, go ahead and then to the right here. *If you are returning to the pub*, turn left on a narrow path that leads out to the road. Turn left and follow the road all the way back. This time, don't cross the field behind the church, but continue on the road and take a peep at the church and its door as you pass. At the road junction, turn left to return to the Exeter Arms.

PLACES OF INTEREST NEARBY

For maps of the forest (including an orienteering map) and lots of information, call at the Forest Enterprise headquarters at Top Lodge. This is just across the A43 from Wakerley, in **Fineshade Wood** – where there are more marked forest trails and occasional exhibitions in the farm buildings.